ART MATTERS

ART MATTERS

Reflecting on Culture

John Tusa

Methuen

Published by Methuen 1999

3 5 7 9 10 8 6 4 2

First published in the United Kingdom in 1999 by
Methuen Publishing Limited
215 Vauxhall Bridge Road, London SW1V 1EJ

Methuen Publishing Limited Reg. No. 3543167

A CIP catalogue record for this book
is available from the British Library

ISBN 0 413 73890 6

Typeset by Deltatype Ltd, Birkenhead, Merseyside
Printed and bound in Great Britain by
Creative Print and Design (Wales), Ebbw Vale

Contents

Introduction

An article I had written expressing doubts about the direction and sense of purpose behind Labour's arts policy – 'I'm Worried about Tony' – appeared in *The Times* on 11 March 1998. By the time I got into the office that morning, there was a note from Michael Earley at Methuen suggesting that we should meet to discuss a collection of essays on the state of the arts in Britain today. This volume is the result.

A great deal of it had already been written, in the form of speeches or lectures given since becoming Managing Director of the Barbican Centre in November 1995. Other possible chapters were already in the pipeline in the form of booked speaking engagements. Between us, Michael Earley and I rejected some and decided on others that I would write up specially for the book. Finally, when the chosen essays had been identified, it was Michael who grouped them into three sections – Beliefs, Politics, Actions – having perceived a grouping of themes which I might have sensed but had not pinpointed so clearly. It was he who found the book its title. I am grateful to him for his wholehearted commitment to the project and his sharp and enthusiastic understanding of the issues discussed in it.

I am grateful too to the various institutions which provided the opportunity to set out my thoughts about these arts issues. They include the Anglo-Israeli Association ('A New Rhetoric for the Arts'); Battersea Arts Centre ('The Agony and the Ecstasy'); the British Council in Prague ('Culture and Identity'); the University of Portsmouth ('Is there Space for Art?'); the London School of Economics ('The Good Society'); the Marketing Association ('Art for Art's Sake'); Amsterdam Leisure and

Arts Consulting Group ('Marketing and the Arts'); and the Arts
Administration School of City University ('The ABC of
Running an Arts Centre'), our immediate neighbours at the
Barbican, and where I am Visiting Professor.

The main problem with a collection such as this is that
speeches and lectures have their own styles of writing. And since
there is no logical rhyme or reason behind the invitations that
one receives to speak, the same or similar subjects tend to
reappear. To the extent that these chapters have been purged of
the worst of their stylistic excesses of speech, and to the extent
that repetitions have been reduced, though not wholly eliminated, I owe it to my wife, Ann Tusa. She brought her historian's
eye – and the habits of a teacher – to the task of rigorous sub-
editing and judicious rewriting of these chapters. I am grateful for
the time and effort she devoted to them. In the end, an editor
can only do as well as the material put into her hands.

A word on the second section, Politics. Some may think it
rash for anyone involved in the day-to-day life of the British arts
scene to appear to cross swords with its three leaders – the Prime
Minister, the Culture Secretary and the Chairman of the Arts
Council. My own view is that the questions of arts policy today
are so important that everyone has a duty to become involved in
that debate, and I have tried to address the issues and avoid the
personalities. Both Chris Smith and Gerry Robinson set out their
philosophies of arts funding and support in a substantial way. It is
essential that those assumptions should be carefully scrutinised.
That is all that I have tried to do.

Much of what I have written has been informed by my three
and a half years as Managing Director of the Barbican Centre.
During that time I have had unfailing support from my two
Chairmen of the Barbican Centre Committee – first Geoffrey
Lawson and, for the last two and a half years, Mrs Joyce Nash –
and clear advice and strong backing from my immediate
predecessor as Managing Director, the Town Clerk and Cham-
berlain of the Corporation of London, Bernard Harty. The
commitment of the Corporation to the arts in Britain – it is the
third largest funder of the arts after the government and the BBC

– remains one of the unsung and unrecognised features of Britain's arts scene.

Yet these articles are not in any sense about the Barbican Centre. That subject, though fascinating in its own terms, would be too much of an arts microcosm, and in many ways an atypical one at that. They are, however, influenced by the experience of running it and learning about those problems that are common to it and to other arts institutions of many kinds. For more than three years, I have had close involvement at Board level with the Wigmore Hall, English National Opera, and the National Portrait Gallery. The insight into the way that other directors, boards and staff approach a similar raft of challenges has been extremely valuable not only in the way I have run the Barbican but in the knowledge I have gained for this book. The subjects I write about are familiar to any British arts institution, the dilemmas shared ones.

The last three years, too, have seen the reshaping of the Barbican Centre from a site whose chief characteristic was the strength and quality of its two resident institutions – the London Symphony Orchestra and the Royal Shakespeare Company – to one where the Barbican's own promotions – most notably the 'BITE '98' season in the theatre and 'Inventing America' in the concert hall – have created a third leg to our artistic stool. With the recent addition of the Barbican Art Gallery as a full part of the Centre, we are still more solidly poised to realise the potential that exists from housing 'all the arts under one roof', from having two strong resident companies as artistic partners, and from being Europe's largest arts centre.

Throughout these years of reshaping, the Barbican's Director-ate team – Graham Sheffield (Arts), Ernest Newhouse (Finance), Mark Chapman (Operations), Mark Taylor (Commercial), Ruth Hasnip (Public Affairs), Diane Lennan (Personnel) and, most recently, John Hoole (Art Galleries) – have made the hard times manageable and the easier moments enjoyable. I am grateful to them for their professionalism, sense of humour and tolerance.

By a happy coincidence, the image on the cover is of the stage

fittings of the Barbican Theatre. It comes from a colour
transparency and light box by Catherine Yass, whose permission
to use it is gratefully acknowledged. The suggestion that it would
make a suitable cover was made to me by Penny Johnson,
Director of the Government Art Collection who possess the
work in question. My thanks to her for taking the time to give
me some striking options from which to choose.

During the last three years, David Miller of Rogers Coleridge
and White has been assiduous in placing several of these essays
into newspapers and magazines. My thanks to him and to
Deborah Rogers for actively assisting the creation of this
collection.

My PA, Joanna Fyvie, deserves thanks for taking it all in her
stride. Wonderfully efficient, with a memory like an elephant,
she makes a reminder never seem like a nag. For ordering my
time, covering my back, making the phone calls I cannot face,
and generally making life possible, my fond thanks.

Finally, to state the obvious, none of this would be worth
doing if the arts were not simply the most important thing in life.
Everything else pales into insignificance. Standing up for them
matters because Art Matters.

Part One: Beliefs

1 The Arts – Can We Do Without Them?

A nniversaries, those great props of the tired editor, are also fine joggers of the memory. They remind us of time passed, of happenings overlooked, of things achieved. After fifty years, we have the opportunity to put those events into perspective. It is time to get some perspective on the arts in Britain and two major anniversaries help us to do so. Just over fifty years ago, on 12 June 1945, the Arts Council of Great Britain was created. The child of war and of the economist John Maynard Keynes, you might have thought that its half century would have found the arts in Britain bursting to celebrate the achievement of five decades of artistic patronage and development.

Some fifty years ago too, in September 1946, the Director General of the BBC, William Haley, created the Third Programme. That anniversary itself was properly and widely celebrated. It was, after all, the world's first radio network devoted to matters of art, culture and the intellect. Yet there was an angst there, as if honour was being accorded to a monument – grand of course, a tribute to its creators, a brilliant child of its time, but viewed with uncertainty by its present-day inheritors. None of the birthday tributes expressed any confidence that today's BBC would be capable of creating from scratch a Radio 3 of the existing kind or was at all equipped or inclined to do so. Still less would today's market-research-obsessed, focus-group-driven planners create anything remotely resembling the Third Programme on which Haley so confidently chanced his arm. To do so needed an unclouded, confident vision. Few of those praising the Third's birthday, myself included, bothered to conceal their fear that

Radio 3 in a recognisable form would be lucky to exist ten years
from now, or that the existing funding for the BBC's orchestras –
a sure bell-wether of serious cultural commitment – would
survive the decade. A fine anniversary to celebrate, but was it not
also the subtle ending of an era?

There was a similarly dying fall to the marking of the other
great artistic anniversary, that of the Arts Council. In their
annual news conference in October 1996, the then leaders of the
Arts Council of England – Lord Gowrie, the Chairman, and
Mary Allen, the Director General – were in no position to praise
Caesar; they appeared to be preparing to bury him. There was no
great celebration of fifty years of success in developing and
supporting the arts. Instead Gowrie and Allen minced no words
about their fears of the Treasury and its inexorable impending
funding cuts – 'The Ministry of "No" ', according to Gowrie.
They were openly fearful about the consequences for Britain's
major performing companies if a further year of cuts in real terms
was piled onto three previous years of standstill grants, leaving
the recipients to make good the upward drift in inflation. A cut
by any other name would cut as deep. Did the Treasury think arts
organisations did not bleed? The haemorrhage in the arts was
real because it represented the sapping of creative talent, the
ebbing of creative energy, the wilting of creative courage. If the
funding crisis of 1996 looks less acute now than it did then, that
is because the Labour Government's rebasing of arts funding in
the summer of 1998 has provided palliatives; it is too early to say
if they are solutions. Besides, arts crises and arts funding
settlements have their own cyclical pattern and this may, just
may, be one of them. Far more important is the prior question of
whether we need the arts at all; to answer that requires a sense of
time passed, and in retreading the experience of the past, the
footfall of anniversaries can help.

To start with, these calendar landmarks should jolt us by
introducing some perspective. Beset as we are with a pervading
sense of troubles today, we should look back at the last half-
century not in anger and dismay but with wonder at an
extraordinary period of arts renaissance. Fifty years ago there was

no Royal Opera, no English National Opera, and no opera company in Wales, Scotland, the North of England or Ulster. Fifty years ago, there was no Royal Shakespeare Company, no Royal National Theatre, no Royal Court Theatre company. Fifty years ago, there was no Royal Festival Hall, no Barbican Centre, no Symphony Hall in Birmingham, no Orchestra Hall in Glasgow, no Bridgwater Hall in Manchester, no Grand Opera House in Belfast to name only a few.

Fifty years ago, there was no Sainsbury Wing extension to the National Gallery in London, no Museum of Modern Art in Edinburgh, no Burrell Collection in Glasgow, no Tate Gallery in either Liverpool or St Ives. The Courtauld Collection was not housed in Somerset House. Fifty years ago, the suggestion that the Tate might be contemplating a huge additional gallery space in the then still working Bankside power station would have been dismissed as arrogant and unnecessary. Fifty years ago, the prospect that the much-loved Sadler's Wells would act as cradle and midwife to the English National Opera and then be rebuilt and reborn as the nation's dedicated dance house would have been regarded as insanely visionary. The possibility that we as a nation would find ourselves in a position where we could modernise many significant arts buildings from scratch, and often build something entirely new into the bargain, would have been treated as over-heated fantasy.

Writing in 1948, T. S. Eliot was apocalyptic about the future as he viewed the post-war British cultural scene. Standards were lower than at the start of the century, he asserted. 'I see no reason why the decay of culture should not proceed much further and why we may not even anticipate a period, of some duration, of which it is possible to say that it will have no culture.' Today's cultural scene hardly bears out Eliot's gloomy predictions. It is very hard to see why he should have been so pessimistic. For, over the course of the last half-century, something has changed in the way the British regard and treat the arts – and changed hugely for the better.

Yet despite the unexpected glow induced by contemplating these outstanding five decades of achievement, the immediate problems facing the arts today are alarming. They need restating only in broad, but bleak, outline. If grants to arts institutions fail to match inflation then they are cut in real terms. The effect of that cut is not to induce economy into those institutions; it merely condemns them to ultimate financial crisis. That was the all too painful experience of the Thatcher and Major years. Recently there appears to have been some improvement in arts funding. But given the next financial crisis, the reach-me-down Treasury solution will be to put funding onto standstill again, if it is not actually cut. Another crisis will follow automatically, with theatres, orchestras, dance and opera companies cutting costs and activity savagely in order to balance their books. That is one lesson repeatedly taught over the last fifty years.

For cuts in grants always lead to cuts in performances, reductions in quality, weakened activity, more cautious planning, less imagination and risk-taking; less time is devoted to the arts activity, more time spent on fund-raising, budget-balancing, sponsorship-raising and sacking. As a policy, it is not even respectable in economic terms. Pretending that any institution can find what are called 'efficiency gains' on a continual basis year after year is the economics of the peasant's milch-cow. The thrifty peasant boasted to his neighbours that each year he saved money by feeding his cow a bit less fodder. It worked triumphantly well until one day – to the peasant's evident amazement – the cow dropped dead. That is the situation to which most arts institutions are subjected. Do not be surprised when they start to keel over. Remember, too, that during the years when the cow was fed less and less, its constant moos of complaint were disparaged as mere 'whingeing'.

Do not believe anyone who says that the arts are spendthrift. They do not have that option. Most top-class British actors and actresses are paid a weekly wage rather less than the daily charge-out rate of the management consultants constantly inflicted upon them. Most singers – good ones at that – are not paid as Pavarotti or Domingo or Jessye Norman or Angela Gheorghiu are paid. Though, incidentally, if you work in a profession where you are asked to fly from California in order to sing the Count in *Figaro* at a couple of hours' notice, go to the theatre sleepless and jetlagged, and find that you have never even seen your Countess before, then that is surely worth a bob or two.

Most orchestral players are wretchedly paid and get many noughts removed from the fees demanded by the top-rank soloists. For four years, between 1995 and 1999, the rank-and-file players in Britain's best orchestra, the London Symphony Orchestra, accepted a wages standstill because the Arts Council grant was frozen. Nor are audiences, decried as 'middle-class' by some, particularly well-heeled. Most of those who attend plays, concerts, dance, opera or galleries are not paying the super-gala prices for their seats, but sums lower than those for a West End musical or rock show, and well below the cost of a seat at a Premier League football match. Half the seats at the Coliseum, the home of English National Opera, cost less than £25; a seat at West Ham for a Premier League football match is £27. I will not hear a word said against the team I have supported since a boy, but the £25 spent on opera at the Coliseum usually yields more drama and entertainment, not to mention better singing, than at Upton Park. Before the Royal Opera closed, more people went there in a year than went to watch West Ham at home. (The players at Upton Park are almost as international.) What those figures clearly demonstrate is that the idea of the arts as a ghetto of financial or any other kind of privilege simply bears no relationship to who makes up the audiences and what their pleasure costs them.

When the Lottery grant of some £30 million for the redevelopment of Sadler's Wells was announced in October 1995, the press reaction was, sadly, predictable. Photographers were despatched to the evening performance to witness dinner-jacketed nobs landing from their limos, or taking the interval air with their champagne. To their picture editors' chagrin what they found was a dance audience of the young and the black, casually dressed, coolly drinking beer from the bottle – a far cry from the hoped-for image of privileged and subsidised luxury. Few shutters clicked; no pictures appeared thereafter. It was the wrong story. The reality, which the newspapers would not face, is of a vastly diverse, cheerfully informal, seriously inclined, well informed body of people, carefully allocating to the arts the comparatively small sum of money they have available for discretionary spending. Fifty years of increasing the provision of the highest quality arts has created that audience. Oddly, it has not created an equivalent popular acceptance of that fact. The audience, as Lord Gowrie once observed, is not an elite – the arts are not for elites; but they are conducted by elites, by the best, just as any other human activity, sport not least, is conducted by the best.

And, despite insinuations to the contrary, the arts do not make unreasonable demands on the national purse. Some forty years ago, in 1956, an Arts Council pamphlet celebrating its first decade noted that direct funding through the Council was a tiny fraction of the sums directly spent on education, libraries, galleries and museums. If only, it suggested, half of one per cent of that figure were given to the Council, then the resulting princely uninflated total sum of £2$\frac{1}{2}$ million a year would transform the whole position of arts funding. Forty years on, Lord Gowrie ventured a similar proposal. The arts, he suggested in January 1995 at the Royal Society of Arts, should receive one per cent of present total public spending, to be indexed at two per cent a year. That would yield a massive extra £700 million annually. A modest proposal or a mite ambitious; it was undoubtedly visionary. Yet the proposition that even such a sizeable additional grant to the arts might unbalance government expenditure or control of the public finances is too ludicrous to take seriously.

Of course the arts institutions have always wanted more and need more. They want more in order to meet the needs of audiences more effectively. Over fifty years, if any politician took the long view, the arts have used increased expenditure imaginatively, creatively and effectively. At the present juncture, however, though the arts certainly need more money to do their job better, what they most want is what British industry begged successive governments for: stability and predictability so that they can plan ahead and do their job properly. The Blair

Government and the Chancellor of the Exchequer, Gordon Brown, now appear to understand some of industry's argument for these conditions. But the suspicion remains that the need for financial stability for the arts has not yet been fully taken on board. The powers that be do not seem to know that orchestras and opera companies have to plan four or five years ahead, at least as far in advance as major industries. To do so efficiently, they have to know roughly how much money they will have to spend.

However, the true heart of the uneasy national debate about arts funding is not about money as such nor the way it is allocated. The basic problem lies in the public approach towards the arts as a whole. We are faced less with a question of 'how much' to give, than 'whether to give' at all. The shortage of money reflects a fundamental unease about arts provision in its essence. Fifty years on, the case, it seems, has to be made once again, and constantly. 'Why the Arts?' Do we need them? Why do we have to pay for them? Fifty years on, Britain's internal debate about the place of arts in society is as intense, confused and unresolved as it ever was. In his first policy speech, the new Chairman of the Arts Council of England, Gerry Robinson, called for a debate about the arts. It will surely take place but not necessarily on terms that he will like and certainly not on the narrow terms that he so arbitrarily defined.*

As a start to that debate, it is worthwhile returning to the early years. The great and once again fashionable economist, John Maynard Keynes, the first Chairman of the Arts Council, was severely realistic about arts funding. As he offered to pay from his own pocket the first two-thirds of the cost of the new Arts Theatre in Cambridge in 1935, he observed to his wife, Lydia Lopokova: 'The greatest comfort of all, I think, from having money . . . is that one does not need to badger other people for it.' Not for Keynes the need to pester the rich or well-disposed to make good the shortcomings of public provision for the arts. No one now calculates the opportunity cost to British intellectual

* See Chapter Nine.

life if Keynes had had to spend more time fund-raising and less time thinking, lecturing and writing.

For Keynes, it was an article of belief that a university needed a theatre in exactly the same way as the sciences needed laboratories. Only in a theatre could the complicated dependence of drama upon literature, music and design be put to the test and understood. As to the arts as a whole, he saw their justification in philosophical beliefs which held that goodness in society increased as a result of the amount of beauty. While there are many who still subscribe to such beliefs, only the very naive would think that they cut any ice with a Treasury devoted to strict financial prudence, still less that large claims about the absolute value of beauty can be presented without challenge or dispute. An assertion of this kind today would walk straight into the reductive comment: 'Well, since there is so much more of what you call art around, why is there still so much crime today?' Still, those grander and more absolute propositions were good enough in their time and persuasive enough to establish a process of arts funding that still survives – however uncertainly. By contrast, in today's more sceptical, less idealistic world, the more the arts articulate their 'Vision', the less public imagination there is devoted to funding and turning that vision into reality.

Fifty years ago, as Keynes's Arts Council started work, the founders of the BBC Third Programme were wrestling with similar questions about the national need for culture. Vision they had; commitment they would deliver; but doubts they acknowledged. In fact, the continuing internal and external debate about culture and the arts within the BBC mirrored national doubts in precise form. In 1946, the BBC decided to pay a price for culture – too high a price some said even at the time – and insisted that it was a price worth paying. William Haley, the then Director General, said that he saw every civilised nation as a cultural pyramid with 'a lamentable broad base and a lamentable narrow tip'. Yet the pyramid was not a static one, but culturally upwardly mobile. 'My conception was of a BBC through the years – many years – which would slowly move listeners from one stratum of this pyramid to the next.'

If the wish to be open and inclusive is one that we would recognise today, Haley's terms of reference for the new programme (what we would call the Mission Statement in today's jargon) were more austere and unyielding and, in contrast to other comments, appeared to accept the inevitable exclusion of some in his definition of the target listeners: 'The programme is designed to be of artistic and cultural importance. The audience envisaged is one already aware of artistic experience and will include persons of taste, of intelligence, and of education; it is, therefore, selective and not casual, and both attentive and critical.'

Such were the foundations on which a cornucopia of music, talk and drama was unloaded onto a nation which had never enjoyed anything like it before. Haley had no illusions about the likely popularity of the programme. But he and his supporters were supremely self-confident in their values and their concept of culture. No one fifty years ago had to qualify the word by explaining why culture did not mean 'pop' culture, or 'mass' culture or 'lifestyle' culture or 'club' culture. For Haley and the intellectual middle class, it meant the great continuum of inherited Western creative artistic activity of which they were an instinctive part; it required no further definition, as it does today. It certainly required no apology, as it would now. All the terms of the debate were simpler fifty years ago. In a public speech, Haley noted with disdain that 'the surest way to increase the number of listeners is to debase the standards', a statement with powerful echoes today of the debate about 'dumbing down' by constantly lowering expectations of 'what the audience will take'. Reflecting on Haley's comment, the *Newcastle Journal* observed at the time: 'We are, in general, a low-brow rather than a high-brow people. We should aim, at least, at being soundly middle-brow people, with aspirations towards higher planes.' How different social rhetoric is today: at a time when the middle classes, in financial terms, have never been larger, and the manual working classes are almost a thing of the past, few in public life would care to claim anything but some working-class origins and considerable satisfaction with mass tastes.

Haley's view of culture, indeed the general view of culture half a century ago, was far narrower than it is today. We have absorbed some aspects of pop culture into painting, music, literature and dance. While there is proper debate about the way that pop integrates itself, we are more broad-minded in our readiness to extend the frontiers that define art. There is, too, a greater readiness to include influences from around the world into the activities that could once be simply defined as Western culture. Such eclecticism was a long way from the intellectual world of the post-war era.

It remains remarkable that the BBC should create a project like the Third Programme on such confident, almost insouciant foundations. But if there is an overriding explanation for the comparative ease with which Haley could state and win the case for setting up the Third Programme, it is to be found in the unifying experience of the war and the nation's intensified cultural experience during those years.

In 1939, when CEMA, the Committee for the Encouragement of Music and the Arts was created, it was an emergency operation to save the arts from total black-out – literal and metaphorical. Many of its aims were very practical: to keep up public morale; to entertain bored evacuees, shift workers and servicemen waiting for action; to keep artistes in employment; and, almost as an afterthought, to spread knowledge of and enjoyment of the arts themselves. Under the CEMA umbrella, the Old Vic had three touring companies on the road playing one-night stands in town halls, miners' institutes, and factory hostels. In 1940, a travelling exhibition called 'Art for the People' attracted 300,000 visitors during its journey through 80 villages and country towns. By 1944, CEMA provided no fewer than 6,140 concerts of which 840 were symphony concerts. Granted that many of the audiences had nothing else to do, and conceding that not all experienced a sudden conversion to the fine arts, this somewhat forced wartime exposure to them had a revolutionary and lasting effect in building a new national cultural base. From today's perspective, the CEMA initiative has a very *dirigiste* feel to it, paternalist, prescriptive. Yet just as food rationing delivered striking improvements in public health, and utility clothing put decent clothes on the backs of rich and poor alike, CEMA presented good quality to all – and, in so doing, not only broadened public appreciation of the arts but increased people's desire to experience more. A foundation was built.

So successful was CEMA in creating a new audience, that the Arts Council evolved speedily from it as the war ended. Keynes believed that the new council would 'carry the arts throughout the countryside and maintain metropolitan standards' – both ideals that have informed arts policy ever since. Though many today would see his remark as patronising to the regions, for Keynes it only meant sharing access to the best available. Despite his belief in the widespread availability of the arts, Keynes was not, according to Kenneth Clark, 'a man for wandering minstrels and amateur theatricals. He believed in excellence.' Many believed that after the hideous dangers and sufferings of the war, the nation deserved something better. That included the arts. The wartime possibility of death or captivity sharpened the appetite for life and art hugely.

It was against this broader national background of an appetite awakened that the Third Programme was born. Despite constant niggles at the smallness of the audience, and its disproportionate cost – disproportionate, that is, to the rest of radio – the BBC persevered over the decades with a third network of some kind or another, tacking and trimming to the prevailing financial and artistic winds but trying to keep intact a recognisably cultural network with terms of reference beyond those of its more mainstream or populist partners. There were repeated attempts to define why the arts were worth undertaking and continuing. For a while, those definitions changed little.

When a former BBC Controller of Music, Robert Ponsonby, wrote that 'what is unarguable is that the BBC should be unreservedly committed to a radio channel devoted to music and the arts at a discriminating level of quality, intelligence and articulacy', his vocabulary and approach were not that different from Haley's forty years earlier. When, however, the former Controller of BBC Radio 3, Nicholas Kenyon observed in 1998 that 'the tension between highbrow culture and popular culture and the cost of what we do and the number of people who use it' has changed little over fifty years, he exposed the distance still to go before the arts have an assured place in Britain. The future and the nature of Radio 3 will remain the white flag in the nation's cultural tug of war. It is a battle still to be fought, a battle still to be won.

The evidence of the BBC's fifty-year-long internal and public debate about Radio 3 demonstrates that abstract claims for the arts cast in absolute terms have not got them or their argument very far. The unconvinced remain unconvinced. In this respect, the pragmatic, utilitarian British – or is it the English? – are utterly different from their continental cousins. It is as if the British are guilty about supporting the arts, or worse still, simply agnostic. As a result, in the last decade and a half, the arts have jumped through a series of hoops trying to convince the public that they are worth paying for. The process has been often educative, occasionally undignified and ultimately ineffective. The implied case for the last half century that the arts were good in themselves has been rudely set aside as other, and perhaps unsuitable, criteria have been introduced. The fact that they have been imposed at all suggests a general failure by all of us in the arts to justify our *raison d'être* in terms that command political and public support.

The difficulties began in 1983 when the recently created National Audit Office introduced fresh ways of looking at the finances of the arts. Using the still novel criteria of 'economy, efficiency and effectiveness' which it applies without fear or favour to all the institutions it scrutinises, the NAO made Performance Indicators the yardsticks of effectiveness, Forward Plans with Specific Activity Targets the measures of efficiency, and tougher accounting systems the guarantors of economy. We were in a new world. We were no longer the arts, pure and simple, but rather part of a great national cultural industry, just another sector of the economy. The Whitehall managerial revolution did not single out the arts for special attention; its working methods applied to all and sundry.

In 1985, the Arts Council Chairman, William Rees-Mogg, took the hint. Deploying the new managerialism with relish, in his lecture entitled 'The Political Economy of the Arts', Rees-Mogg stated: 'The Arts Council gives the best value for money in job creation of any part of the state system . . . The arts are to Britain what the sun is to Spain.' It was a good try but failed to notice two facts: first, the Thatcher Government was less interested in job creation (the traditional cry of the unions) and only in wealth creation; and, second, everybody in Spain liked and enjoyed the sun which comes free in any case.

In 1985, the Arts Council tried again, proclaiming the arts to be 'The Great British Success Story', and issuing 'an invitation to the nation to invest in the arts'. Unlike all other privatisation issues, that prospectus was distinctly undersubscribed. Nobody felt inclined to 'Tell Sid' to put his money in there in a hurry. In 1986, the Council tried still harder. 'Partnership: Making Arts Money Work Harder.' The language used to argue the arts case changed. We no longer promoted concerts, mounted exhibitions or put on a production of a play; we delivered 'product'. Gone were the days when visitors went to galleries, audiences attended concerts or the theatre; they were all 'customers'. An arts institution – if it knew what was good for it – 'delivered product to the customer'. Subsidy or public patronage were out-of-date words; the arts were looking for 'investment'. In these new cant terms, a well-managed arts institution would deliver 'a properly focused and researched product, appropriately diverse for its particular clients, consistent with its vision and targets while working to externally agreed and objectively measurable performance indicators'. By 1998, the Arts Council Chairman, Gerry Robinson, was impatiently demanding an end to 'an assembly of wish lists from every part of the arts constituency'. He insisted on a 'limited amount of deliverable priorities'.

The trouble is that – then and now – the language is all wrong. It is not merely that it is not ours; it is not appropriate to our activity. A member of an audience expects good service but is buying an experience – a very different thing. A product is a predictable, quantifiable object which is expected to perform jobs, tasks or functions. A play, dance, opera, exhibition or concert offers something varied, variable, untried or tested, often unpredictable and occasionally experimental. But the real trap in the dialogue of the 1980s occurred with the word 'investment'. As the arts world queued up with its list of proposed investments, there was one response: 'What is the return on the investment?' To which the only answer was: 'There is no return on the investment in the sense that the word is properly understood.' Back came the reply: 'Then why are you asking us to invest in you at all?' Words matter. Vocabulary must be appropriate and we will get nowhere by using words which conceal what we are and why we do what we do.

Using managerial vocabulary has never yet produced great art. History suggests the reverse. Supposing Diaghilev had had to work within the parameters of such vocabulary, would he have created *Firebird*, *Petrouchka* or *The Rite of Spring*? What would the twentieth century have been without the music that Diaghilev commissioned from Stravinsky, or the designers like Bakst or choreographers like Massine and Fokine who mounted the ballets? Theirs was the dialogue of art – while Diaghilev was always a canny businessman. If the basic language is that of business, can the result be art? Occasionally, perhaps, but only if you mind your concepts, and realise that business theories are instruments rather than ends. Too often in recent years, the arts have behaved as if they will only be taken seriously if they lean over backwards and pretend to be what they are not. We may have some of an industry's characteristics, but we remain essentially different. Unless that difference is stated and restated, then the wind will change and we will end up thinking of ourselves as a business, behaving like one too and forgetting our responsibilities to art.

Let us do a deal. We in the arts will not resist the business jargon that has been forced upon us. It is not difficult to use; all too easy in fact. Many of its principles do help you to run the theatre, the orchestra or the gallery in a business-like manner. But we will only talk like a business if our interlocutors accept that we are different. We will learn their tricks and not shy away from some of their vocabulary; but they in return must understand what distinguishes and separates us.

The arts continue to wriggle with a series of instrumental arguments – all turning on the proposition that they should be supported not because of what they are but because of the impact they have. In 1986, the Arts Council's 'Partnership' document held up the arts as an instrument of urban renewal. Inner cities would be revived, cultural industries would grow as a result, and employment would follow. True enough. Education would improve too. As arts and musical education faltered in schools, arts institutions must carry out emergency, remedial work. Without an education programme, would there be an audience in a decade's time? This case for the arts turns them into a kind of super-welfare industry, another arm of Treasury economic regeneration policy, a part of the enterprise culture. If they are to be all these things, is there any room or time for being what they should be: institutions and people striving for the highest possible artistic achievement?

By 1988, the economic argument was in full flood. A Policy Studies Institute paper called 'The Economic Importance of the Arts in Britain' recorded a gross turnover from the arts sector of £10 billion; it employed 500,000 people directly; accounted for 1.28% of gross domestic product; and ranked fourth in the list of invisible export-earners. Think, too, how much the state earned in VAT and taxes, in taking people out of costly unemployment. Later still, the arts were presented as a key component in the transition from an industrial to a post-industrial society, in the evolution from a working society to a leisure society, and in the generation of economic multiplier effects – if a successful theatre opens, the nearby leisure and dining quarter follows.

These arguments – barring a few quibbles about what was included in the figures – were neither inaccurate nor invalid. At the time they seemed novel, impressive and weighty. Even so, they were inadequate for raising arts funding onto a new level, where stability and predictability could be relied upon. Worst of all, the arts had fallen into the trap of arguing on the other side's ground and terms. They were bound to lose. They still begged the question, 'Why the arts at all?' Of course, they were useful 'as parts of the economy' but other great industries that had once justified themselves by creating a lot of jobs had been closed; why should the arts be special? Over the last fifty years, the arts scene has been transformed and for the better; yet one thing has not changed: the fundamental questioning of the arts and the demand that if they claim to be special, they must make the claim for special treatment stick. Everyone involved in the arts must make their own attempt at such a justification.

Here is my own attempt.

The arts matter because they are universal; because they are non-material; because they deal with daily experience in a transforming way; because they question the way we look at the world; because they offer different explanations of that world; because they link us to our past and open the door to the future; because they work beyond and outside routine categories; because they take us out of ourselves; because they make order out of disorder and stir up the stagnant; because they offer a shared experience rather than an isolated one; because they encourage the imagination, and attempt the pointless; because they offer beauty and confront us with the fact of ugliness; because they suggest explanations but no solutions; because they present a vision of integration rather than disintegration; because they force us to think about the difference between the good and the bad, the false and the true. The arts matter because they embrace, express and define the soul of a civilisation. A nation without arts would be a nation that had stopped talking to itself, stopped dreaming, and had lost interest in the past and lacked curiosity about the future.

The question of why the arts matter cannot be answered on the back of a Kellogg's Cornflakes packet – or if it can, then I have certainly not won the competition. Matthew Arnold defined the arts as 'the best that has been thought and said in the world', and of course the best sung, acted, danced, painted and performed in any way. William Blake, quoted by Robert Hewison in his excellent book *Culture and Consensus*, stated: 'Let it be no more said that the States encourage Arts; for it is the Arts that encourage States.' Let the present-day British state allow itself a moment of encouragement by permitting the arts to flourish. It does not involve a huge financial risk; the experience of the last fifty years demonstrates the effectiveness with which the arts have created an entirely new landscape in Britain for creativity. Rather, any risk involved to the British economy or the well-being of the state lies entirely in under-providing for the arts today and having to pick up the pieces tomorrow.

Not long ago, I was discussing such ideas with a dinner companion whom I had never met before. Was she worried about the arts today? She said that her recurring nightmare, one that she had dreamed throughout her life, was of a darkness into which broken fragments of pictures and musical instruments were hurtling. Through it she felt a personal sense of disintegration. I believe that a society where pictures and music – and everything else in the great body of the arts – have gone to pieces through neglect or indifference would be darkness indeed.

More recently, I asked a distinguished British composer what would happen if there was a moratorium on the playing or performance of music composed before 1920. Would we not, I suggested, return to it after the moratorium with a renewed sense of its value and the essential part it plays in our lives? No, he replied bleakly; we would never return to it at all.

Are things so perilously balanced between continuity and extinction? I do not believe so. But we have both to defend the arts and, better still, explain them in ways that do justice to them for what they are rather than diminish them. T S. Eliot was wrong fifty years ago when he was struck by the utter barrenness of the cultural outlook in Britain. We should not assume that without passionate and determined advocacy he might not be right in the next fifty years.

2 The Arts in the Twenty-First Century – The Agony or the Ecstasy?

I have a dream, or is it a nightmare? Of a world without arts – and therefore without arts centres. It will come true in the next century, probably within a few years of its starting. Do not worry then about how to run arts centres, how to programme them, market them, or publicise them. Do not fret about audiences – they will be 'customers'; do not anguish about promoting plays, dance or concerts – they will be merely 'product'; do not agonise about audience response – concentrate on 'customer satisfaction'; do not worry about how well you are doing – just ask whether you are meeting your 'performance indicators', 'measuring outcome against promised deliverables'. If you devise an arts season, you will first have to show that you have a 'viable exit strategy'. As you plan your programmes, never forget to ask yourself if you are adequately 'penetrating the core repertoire'. If the audience liked something once, all you will have to do is give it to them again. Undermined by such vocabulary, sapped by such assumptions, in the twenty-first century art will be obsolete. So will arts centres.

There are various pressing reasons for taking such a pessimistic view. None of them are fanciful. All of them relate to theories, practices and principles that exist today and will gain ground and strength over the years. As the arts wilt under the relentless pressure from the experience of the mass electronic media, so the charge of elitism – in the sense of social and financial exclusiveness – will grow. The more elitist the arts are accused of being – no matter how unfairly – the more difficult it will be to justify spending government money – the taxpayers' money, after all – on them. Market testing and consumer research will erode and undermine artistic judgement as it is enfeebling editorial vision in the BBC. Targets will be set for attendances at arts events. Research will establish what sort of programmes will hit the bull's-eye. Events that clearly miss will be excluded because they stop the business plan being fulfilled. Independent artistic activity will be undermined. So will the taking of risk.

Other current trends point further to such pessimistic conclusions. The funding of arts activities will be determined by quotas – regional quotas, educational quotas, ethnic quotas, disabled quotas, interest group quotas. Anyone who claims to be excluded from the range of activities mounted by an arts centre will be listened to more than those who are satisfied with them. Conversely – but at the same time – unless the provision of arts and the satisfaction derived from them are demonstrated as being universal, they will be deemed to be discriminatory and inadequate.

Above all, the arts – like education – will have to be judged 'relevant'. Unless their utility and immediate comprehensibility to the broad public is demonstrated, then the time, space and money spent on them will be questioned or eliminated. Just as dangerous: arts organisations will have to demonstrate the value of the 'opportunity cost' of the various assets devoted to them. Since those investments can invariably get quicker, surer, more obvious returns from other activities, the arts will sink under the weight of their perceived failure to optimise the use of scarce resources.

So the arts and arts centres, previously cut loose from their intellectual moorings by current ways of thinking, will ebb away in a tide of indifference compounded with actual hostility. They already stand naked and without defence in a world where what cannot be measured is not valued; where what cannot be predicted will not be risked; where what cannot be controlled will not be permitted; where what cannot deliver a forecast outcome is not undertaken; where what does not belong to all will be allowed to none. That is the agony.

For we have lost a vocabulary and an area of permitted public discourse where values are valued rather than costed; where inspiration is regarded as heaven-sent rather than an unacceptable risk. Instead, we have a materialistic debate where the immaterial is dismissed as pretentious rather than welcomed as essential; where art for art's sake is pigeon-holed as a personal obsession rather than recognised as a vital social ingredient; where the public good is dismissed as a chimera so long as it cannot be quantified on a balance sheet.

But when my nightmare/dream comes true, there will of course still be ecstasy, or whatever its latest chemical form happens to be. Plenty of that. Immediate, constant, diversionary, entertaining, in ever growing intensity in ever growing forms, on an ever growing number of occasions.

Of course, these are all deliberate, provocative exaggerations, aren't they? Not altogether. I am also deadly serious, and so should we all be, about the dangers that exist in the public debate where we have to defend, promote and justify the activities of the arts. It is not that anyone involved wants to buck the currently predominant managerial culture – we do not. It is not difficult to learn. Everyone in the arts above all has a pressing need and obligation to use the little money they have as well as they can. But managerialism should be a tool rather than an end; a method rather than an absolute; a rule of thumb rather than a tablet of stone; a system of analysis rather than a panacea for every problem. If applied without discrimination, managerial vocabulary and methods threaten to swamp the work that they are, overtly, intended to support. They become the master not the servant. They are a necessary part of our lives but are far from sufficient in themselves to make a good arts centre or to allow great art to be created.

Even once that assumption is accepted, once the high priests of managerialism and their highly-priced acolytes, the consultants, are put in their rightful place, the questions anyone involved in running an arts centres must answer in the next century are legion. They can be presented as a set of antithetical challenges that must be addressed and if possible resolved: the claims of Continuity versus the attractions of Novelty; the demands of Memory versus the attractions of Sensation; the calm of Apollo versus the frenzy of Dionysus; the nagging of Curiosity versus the lure of Reassurance; the necessity of Diversity versus the ease of Homogenisation. Where will we define the role and purpose of arts centres in relation to these philosophical co-ordinates?

Continuity versus Novelty. I choose the word 'novelty' deliberately and carefully. I do not mean 'innovation', which I define as the continuous building on, and evolution of, a past continuum of creative work and activity. Novelty is something very different; the pursuit of the merely new, the strange, the curious, with little or no reference to and sometimes a total rejection of the past. This kind of novelty is pursued for its own sake rather than as a new way of listening, of opening minds, or intensifying experience. Arts centres will have the choice or necessity of deciding the balance between continuity and innovation on one side and sheer novelty on the other. They will be coerced into pursuing novelty precisely because it is unencumbered by the past and because its pursuit and presentation can be engaged in without the bore of referring to or learning about the past.

No tradition of the arts – at least in the Western world – has been able to survive without taking forward what has been achieved and developing it in new and untried directions, in short without innovation. To date, most arts organisations have kept a balance between the performance and the maintenance of the great canon of Western art-works and the process of extending that tradition. A sense of history and the historical achievement is not incompatible with innovation, rather it plays an essential part in it. I asked the celebrated German composer, Hans Werner Henze, an arch-modernist to many, where he saw his musical roots. He replied unhesitatingly: 'My roots are with Beethoven!' What is under increasing threat is devotion to, respect for, and teaching of the centuries of artistic achievement which underpin all art forms. The past is regarded by too many people as just that – gone, and so different from modern sensibilities, experience and outlook as to be irrelevant to behaviour and understanding. The wholly new on the other hand is immediate, sensational, value-free, unencumbered by comparison, and skilfully tailored to contemporary sensibilities. It rejects the validity of any critical comparison as being too deferential to a rejected past. The wholly new deflects any suggestion of value judgement with the disarming defence that whatever is done is intended ironically, knowingly and therefore incorporates its own judgements within itself.

As the education process seems to place an ever greater emphasis on personal expression rather than systematic learning, absorbing knowledge of the historical artistic canon seems more and more burdensome, less a pillar of support, and more a dead-weight of needless obligation. The audience for the artistic presentation of the historical canon and those activities that grow from it will wither because less has been taught and therefore less is understood. Arts centres have to choose where they stand in this process and defend their decisions.

That means they will also have to reconcile the conflicting demands of Memory and Sensation. Will arts centres carry in themselves a sense of the past rather than a mere indulgence in the present, deliberately retaining awareness of tradition rather than a monochrome existence in the everyday? Arts centres are not just places where a nod to the past is an intrinsic and essential part of the work of the present, but where a knowledge of what has been done in the past is an essential and precious building brick in the creation of art today. At the very least, knowing where to pick and choose in the immeasurably rich traditions of the past should be part of the atmosphere sustained and presented by an arts centre. Those who think they can dispense with any knowledge of the artistic past are as shallow as they are presumptuous. Will arts centres hold to such a position in the face of those who insist that today we know everything, that it is easily stored on a computer, is readily available to everybody and that this obviates the need for any sustained or organised engagement with or understanding of the past?

While they decide, they will have to bear in mind a tension that exists between two other demands – those of Curiosity and Reassurance. Arts centres know that much of the best that they must offer in order to justify survival will challenge, extend understanding, develop experience, and be driven by innovation and curiosity. But will they offer it? For this is a difficult pitch to make. It assumes a willingness on the part of audiences to reach beyond the familiar in form and subject matter. Elsewhere, much of contemporary mass culture is driven by an overwhelming wish to provide the blandly reassuring. Elsewhere, too, much that is trivial is excused or justified on the grounds that everyone knows that 'it is all a giggle' or ironic.

And while all the conflicts are being mediated, all the opposing claims met, another feud tears the arts centres. Never mind the false gods, with which true god will they stand? With calm Apollo or with frenzied Dionysus? In 1968, the musical *Hair* declared the dawning of a new age – the age of Aquarius, of feelings and instinct, of non-rationality and freedom from restraint or inhibition. Today, we can express that trend differently through classical mythology rather than astrology. For society has rediscovered the appeal of Dionysus. Extreme self-expression, encouraged into ecstatic states by ever new classes of designer drugs, is an increasingly accepted – or at least unchallenged – form of leisure activity. The escape from reason does not have to be chemical. Group hysteria, cultural alcoholia, new instant 'religions' such as 'Dianism' are just as attractive, distracting and 'alternative'. Whatever the nature of the original stimulus, mind and thought are deliberately abandoned in a regular, systematic indulgence in non-cerebral activities. An alleged natural urge for togetherness is pursued and delivered in an atmosphere of often synthetically induced, physical ecstasy. The fallible, imperfect, inadequate but precious human interactions that make up true community are rejected and substituted by a beguiling chemical buzz of illusion, noise, electronic sensory deprivation and ultimately by delusion.

The Apollonian qualities – rational, pensive, cool, inquiring, reserved, dispassionate – are in much more limited demand. Acknowledging the fact that all art involves a constant interplay between the two spirits, it has to be accepted that by comparison with the unbridled Dionysiac atmosphere of much of today's leisure and entertainment world, the arts, even at their most uninhibited, fall squarely into Apollo's camp. Here there is an underlying belief in qualities other than instant, constant and unreflecting self-gratification. Where will arts centres ultimately place themselves between these two competing gods? Will they decide that unless they offer some of the atmosphere of clubbing, they will be bypassed and rejected? If they do not, they must bear in mind the fate of the opponents of Bacchus in the *Bacchae* who were ultimately torn apart in a frenzy by the Maenads. Those who totally ignore Bacchus/Dionysus do so at their peril.

So if my dream or nightmare does come true, will purpose-built premises for the arts be value-free zones because the determination of worth has been abandoned on the grounds that attempting to separate the good from the bad is too difficult, unfashionably prescriptive or even allegedly intellectually oppressive? In a society where values are relative, why should anyone bother with matters such as the good and the bad? Or will they keep up a commitment to a flow of value-led activity strongly rooted in the past even as it risks disturbing its audiences?

How, too, will we meet the demands of Diversity versus Homogenisation? Are we to rest content with a world made safe for Macfood and Waltculture and Rupertnews and Tedvision? Will we lie down meekly before the warriors of globalisation who impose a new totalitarianism of taste, thought, experience and views decking out self-serving economic arguments in the pseudo-democratic clothing of freedom and choice? Or will arts centres speak out for and make possible the practice, the expression of the local, the particular, the individual, the differentiated, while rejecting the formulaic that is the trademark of the global endeavour? True art is universal but not homogenised – its diversity being one element in its richness. Global culture snuffs out categories of artistic endeavour as surely as global enterprise threatens the bio-diversity of natural species.

Such are the questions that really underlie all of our activities and challenge all our assumptions in the future. How we solve them will vary from individual to individual and flow from decisions as to what the arts are about. Why do we bother with them? Why do millions of viewers, listeners, audience members engage in them at all? We all have our private answers and we should make them rather more public. We must reclaim the area of public discourse on the arts from the managers and consultants. How would I do it? Something like this.

Art is about searching and sometimes finding; it defines pain and sorrow and sometimes softens them; it is about exploring confusion and defining disorder; it is about sharing the private and listening to silence; it is lasting but not immediate; it is valuable but priceless; it is based in the past but reaches for the future; it is free to anybody but may not be used by everybody; it is universal though it may be attacked as exclusive; it is diverse and not homogenised; it resists categories and makes connections across them. Art is all the things that the rest of life is not.

I cannot conceive of a century, a decade, a year, a minute of the future without it. Surely, neither can anyone else if they think about it seriously. But the dream will end as a nightmare unless we take it seriously.

3 When I Hear the Word Culture, I Reach for My Identity

Put together two British arts directors today and they talk of money. The British arts scene is overwhelmed by issues of funding, with the micro questions of subsidy and the macro questions of survival. These problems are obsessive, corroding, destructive and inward-looking. The prospect of hanging may concentrate a man's mind wonderfully, but the prospect of cultural extinction concentrates the mind on nothing useful. Above all, the induced parochialism is particularly sad. The importance of arts and culture in the political scene, and their valuable contribution to the European dimension, are easy to overlook. As an integral part of the culture and history of Europe, we are constantly linked with our European colleagues in a vast nexus of arts exchanges, activities and projects. Yet we seldom reflect on these connections and their value both in the narrow cultural sense and in the contribution they make to the wider European debate.

Defining European cultural identity is a challenge of its own. Even without too specific a definition, thinking about the contribution that existing cultural experience makes to the political task of forging a new Europe is worthwhile, if only because it forces us to raise our horizons beyond our own seemingly ever-present miseries. (By the by, I use the word 'forging' with reluctance and not only because it is a part of official Eurospeak. Its overtones of Stalinist-Leninist brute force in the shaping of events and institutions is too uncomfortable for my own evolutionary taste.)

These thoughts were sharpened by listening to Eurocrats and Euro-enthusiasts at a conference in Prague in March 1998, organised by the British Council. From Lithuania in the Baltic to Slovenia in the Adriatic, the new democracies of the former socialist bloc are desperate to become members of the European Union. For Eurocrats, though, keenness to join the Club is not enough. Without commitment to the ideal, membership would be as shallowly rooted as that of Irish 'stockpot Protestants' who changed their religion in famine-struck Ireland in the nineteenth century not because of a sudden conversion of faith but because it was better than starving. As Eurocrats wrestle with the task of creating true adherence to the European Union in the countries of Central and Eastern Europe, the notion that a millennium or so of European cultural activity might be a good way of reinforcing and popularising the process of widening and deepening Europe has not featured strongly in what has been an overwhelmingly politicised process.

For Eurocrats, the bedrock idea of 'being European' centres upon dedication to the rule of law, human rights and democracy. There is no difficulty about this 'motherhood and apple pie' concept, except that many countries in the former socialist camp still do not enjoy motherhood or apple pie in nourishing quantities. Beyond this, joining and identifying with the new European institutions – the European Parliament, Court of Human Rights, and European Commission – are regarded as almost as important in creating that broader European consciousness. But the thought that Europe's sheer cultural homogeneity might be used to build European identity struck this collection of Eurocrats gathered in Prague with considerable surprise. Does Europe, in the Brussels sense, have an underused instrument for creating union: Europe's common culture? I think it does.

There is a second, more challenging question. If culture is called into play in the political arena, could the livelier sense of a European identity help to set into perspective some of its destructive ethnic rivalries? A sense of a European culture might achieve two apparently contradictory aims; to protect local cultures from being swallowed up in the global mass and to prevent those local cultures themselves from turning inward, rancid and excessively particular, by placing them firmly in a

larger European context. That larger framework would serve to
reassure rather than to overwhelm these smaller cultural entities.

For a start, what is the cultural experience that binds us
together? From the Atlantic to the Urals, as President de Gaulle
used to tease us by saying, Europe has been characterised over
many centuries by a broad unity of artistic experience. From
Monteverdi to Haydn to Dvořak to Borodin to Debussy, to name
but a handful, European composers have written to common
rules of structure and harmony. Some of it is better than other,
but the evolving language of music is universally taught,
universally written down, and universally comprehensible across
all linguistic barriers. It is playable and played by performers of
any nationality, and heard and understood by every nation in
Europe and most races under the sun. It is an extraordinary
shared means of expression and communication.

Theatrically, the stage language and conventions of Chekhov
or George Bernard Shaw or Schiller or Calderon are generally
recognised and enjoyed. For centuries playwrights of all nations
have drawn on the artistic tap-root that is Greek drama. The
European novel embraces everything from Tolstoy, Dostoevsky,
Flaubert, Cervantes, Thomas Mann and Jane Austen. Within
that unity, there are important differences of sensibility and
subject matter. No English writer could have written *Crime and
Punishment*; no Russian writer would have cared to write *Sense
and Sensibility*; no German author could have conceived of *Don
Quixote*. All these authors reflect their nation, class and culture.
Yet, their works are recognisably European, in the sense that the
Tale of Genji, written by the Lady Murasaki in eleventh-century
Japan, is not accessible, enthralling though it is.

In the case of music, the twentieth-century avant-garde takes
its own national forms. Its well-spring was a single controversial
one: the twelve-note serialism of the Second Viennese School of
Webern, Berg and Schoenberg. Contemporary experimentalism
draws from a wider range of sources. But the difference between
the collagist Russian Alfred Schnittke and the jazz-influenced
Briton Mark-Anthony Turnage, is more personal and stylistic
rather than fundamental. Even minimalism – which some would

see as an American creation – turns out to have many forms in different countries, with both Lithuania – in the person of Arvo Paart – and Britain – in the shape of John Tavener – producing composers of an ecstatic, religious, mystical bent, using many of the forms and tricks of minimalism. Arvo Paart is very popular in Britain; he is part of the European experience, the European musical identity. Tavener, though very English, writes music that is fundamentally shaped by his conversion to Greek Orthodoxy. His universality stems from his absorption of the very particular influences derived from another culture and religion.

Europe's composers use a common language and notation, which permit the widest range of individual style, local characteristics and national voices. They have a clear European identity within which they can express themselves in a variety of often extremely nationalistic and local forms. A good thing too: no one would want to listen to a Euro-composer, working to a compositional policy issued by the EU's Cultural Affairs Directorate – someone who might be defined as having the sense of fun of a German, the organisation of an Italian, the experimentalism of a Belgian, and the cosmic gloom of an Englishman. The strength of the European creative musical community derives precisely from its diversity of national and regional expression.

So, too, with musical performance. It is still possible to hear the distinctive and thrilling bray and rasp of Russian brass from the St Petersburg Philharmonic; the authentically woody tone of Czech clarinets; the deliberately tubby inflection of German horns. Each subtly indicates who you are listening to, each expresses a particular voice, perhaps even the national soul. Every orchestra plays the same notes, but the sense and sound, the shaping of phrase, the feeling for rhythm they communicate are distinctive, particular, local. Only Viennese players instinctively hold back the first beat in the bar of a waltz. Few non-French orchestras float the long lines of French melody as effortlessly as their nationals do. No one would have as their first choice an Italian orchestra playing Beethoven, Germans playing Rossini, or French playing Tchaikovsky. There is nothing chauvinistic in this; it merely reflects the joy of European variety, like the delight to be had in the differences of European scenery and the very different feelings each evokes. You can love both the Lake District and the Alps, the Fens and the Po Valley, the Loire and the Danube. Each is different but each is part of the European landscape.

Yet precious though the diversity in musical performance may be, it is increasingly at risk from homogenisation by the internal and the international market. The analogy is with carrots or potatoes in supermarkets. Customers, so supermarkets tell us, demand vegetables of a convenient, nice, uniform shape and size, not something twisted, odd, perhaps tasty and showing the occasional blemish and crust of soil to prove they originated in a garden. Yet customers – so supermarkets are reluctantly discovering – want taste, want variety, want fruit when it is in season. The public's interest in difference rather than sameness is strong and resilient and may be about to make itself truly felt in the marketplace, whether vegetable or cultural.

In the musical supermarket, conductors are cosmopolitan and peripatetic and may be upset by regional quiddity; recording managers judge performances by their acceptability for an international audience; orchestral players travel across national boundaries and mix what they hear with what they instinctively do. All are forces for bland homogenisation into a world identity, a global style of playing, with the essential interest and the character of the local sound in danger of being lost in the process. Despite the existing differences noted above, who in a blind test could honestly and immediately distinguish a British from a Czech or an American orchestra playing Beethoven today?

However, while these are powerful forces for harmonising the musical experience (in the Brussels sense of 'harmonisation'), to identify them and be anxious about them is not an argument for sticking to wholly particularist expressions of cultural identity – diving into the nearest minority bolt-hole and pretending the global developments have gone away. For the forces of globalisation do not have to be forces for sterile uniformity; rather they can produce even greater variety than the local scene could ever achieve by itself.

To be purely practical, the economics of artistic entrepreneurship demand the creation of multinational co-ventures made for performance at a series of arts festivals around the world. Peter Brook's innovative production of *Don Giovanni* at the Aix-en-Provence Festival in 1998 was seen in umpteen countries thereafter. The American minimalist Philip Glass's three-dimensional theatre piece *Monsters of Grace*, an attempt to define the nature of opera in the next century, was a co-production between ten festivals and theatres. The leading innovators on the international festival circuit – Robert Wilson, Robert Lepage, Peter Sellars – have to assemble international funding years in advance before creating the piece itself. Not for nothing are these ventures universally called 'projects'.

While such artistic confections carry their own dangers within them – dangers of preciosity, self-indulgence, a drive to the neurotically experimental – there is no doubt that such cross-breeding yields work that sticking to comfortable national spheres could not deliver. No single venue can mount such ambitious ventures by itself, and each tends to make a virtue of its financial need by deliberately seeking blends of international spice for its programmes.

More fundamentally, creators themselves increasingly want to cross cultural boundaries, to find inspiration in other traditions. For example: the American Philip Glass, in his misleadingly labelled 'opera' *Monsters of Grace*, combined state-of-the-art computer-generated, three-dimensional images with settings of poems by a thirteenth-century Persian mystic, Jelaluddin Rumi. This work defies definition, by genre or by music. Its very freedom from national categories makes it available as a source of experimentation from which all can learn – from both its successes and its failures – and develop.

There are other cases of this trend to hand. The Chinese-American composer Tan Dun has set the words of a sixteenth-century Chinese opera, *Peony Pavilion*, and counterpointed them with a tale of modern love in a production by the radical

American director Peter Sellars. The Romanian director Sylviu Purcarete has adapted and reinterpreted the ancient Greek *Oresteia* in twentieth-century terms. The Japanese director Yukio Ninagawa has created a version of *Hamlet* which is set in a Japanese theatre and uses occasional Kabuki techniques, but which tells one more about sixteenth-century English thinking and politics than any recent home-grown production. Again, seven contemporary American playwrights recently reset the emotions, loves and spirit of Shakespeare's sonnets in playlets about present American social and sexual tensions. Grounded though they were in the original text, they flew beyond it to intensify one's awareness of the timeless human understanding captured by the sonnets themselves.

The lesson is clear. These national artists are all looking to universal themes and inspirations for their own work, while remaining recognisably American, Japanese or Romanian in their basic approach. They are not offering a homogenised version of theatre which anyone can understand because the differences have been ironed out. Rather, they show how strong individual creation can be when it is rooted in strong, national terms of reference and blends them with international influences.

Conversely, there is an alternative contemporary trend in the arts world which celebrates the local by presenting it to an international audience. It is almost obligatory for any festival worthy of the name to draw inspiration from, or to take note of, ethnic artistic performance from around the world. The 1998 City of London Festival included performances by Australian Aborigines, Trinidadian steel bands, Southern Indian temple-dancers, Canadian Inuit throat singers.

This presents a teasing paradox. All these groups represent utterly distinct ethnic, racial or community cultures. As such they are lauded, admired and held up as worthy of study and even imitation. It is precisely because they are not part of mainstream European culture that we are invited to listen to them, respect what they exemplify and enjoy what they have to offer. Implicitly, they are also offered as a rebuke to the weight, authority, unity and consistency of the European artistic canon.

Should we apologise for our shared European inheritance, for its sheer quantity, its historical venerability, its dazzling variety and creativity? To do so would be preposterous, unnecessary and unwise. Not least, the very existence of this unquestionable European experience should form an essential counterpoint to the current political turmoil in the former Eastern Bloc, where the drive to ever smaller national and political units, and the attendant rancour and bloodshed, is one of the greatest threats to post-communist European stability.

What can creative culture offer to the continent that nurtured it? What can it contribute by way of analgesic in the messy course of giving birth to new European identities? I believe that there are at least four areas which will repay observation and could illumine the otherwise cheerless legal, institutional and political mechanics of European integration.

For a start, a culture as broad and historically deep-seated as the common European one cannot lurk in the ethnic or community particularism described above. True, folk-song has inspired composers as great and fertile as Kodály and Bartók and Stravinsky; true it provides recognition, reassures with familiarity and gives pleasure. Yet today's composers find inspiration in the great world outside as much as in local tradition. So do audiences. Europe has gone beyond mere folksiness, it is too mature and complex a civilisation to take refuge in such naive simplicities. Having said this, any culture that ignores its local origins totally loses part of its basic self.

For the process is a two-way one. Local cultures deserve and have their place; they must not be trampled on. They are like biological species whose massive diversity underpins the eco-system. Many are prone to destruction by globalisation and seem too weak in the European experience to survive. We suppress them at our peril and to our loss, though how they can be strengthened naturally rather than artificially remains a problem. The experience of Irish governments in trying to preserve the Gaeltacht in its language and traditional way of life suggests that the job is just as difficult as breeding pandas in captivity.

But the contribution of culture spreads even further. National cultures have a huge political significance and a proven track record of being more effective at preserving democracy and democratic freedoms than political institutions devised for the purpose. Stalin could ignore legal or constitutional restraints and send political elites to the firing squad or the gulag and did so with devastating effect. He could terrify Shostakovich but could still not stop him writing music that serves as a blistering commentary on the dictator and all his works. Soviet despots could keep an iron grip on the media and the book trade; they could not stem the flow of samizdat publication by dissident writers or the outpouring of new novels and poems recited in a million kitchens throughout their empire. The KGB could consign their victims to remote Siberian exile; they had no control over the only exile that mattered, the 'internal exile' of the mind into which Soviet dissidents migrated, and where ideological thought-control had no dominion.

The political suppression of national cultures was a more stubborn problem. The Leninist-Stalinist policy towards the irksome nationalities that made up the Soviet Union was to authorise them in carefully sanitised forms, in what became discredited as 'folkloristic manifestations'. Here, every maiden and her partner existed in a world of fixed smiles, swirling ethnic, multi-petticoated skirts, stamping boots, relentlessly cheerful rhythms and rigidly restricted forms of innovation. This culture was not an expression of national identity; it was a fake substitute for it. It bought the regime some time but it gained no consent.

Ultimately, true national self-expression had the last word over the bogus Stalinist version. Let that be a warning to anyone who thinks that a huge and complex political unit (such as the Soviet Union was or the European Union is today), can have an 'official' unified culture. For genuine autonomous cultures are an essential safety valve for some, though not all, of the tensions that exist in all large units. In pre-1989 Poland, it was the cultural and religious independence of the Roman Catholic Church that acted as the core of resistance to the illegitimacy of Polish communist rule. Once the Party had to concede to the

Church a dual role in the social existence of the country, they had in effect lost the political and intellectual battle for minds.

In Czechoslovakia, the cultural resistance was more oblique but ultimately just as effective over time. It took the form of irony, self-deprecation and a typically Schwejkian form of stubborn, apparently uncomprehending resistance to authority. The satirising of lumpen communist dictatorship, the constant laughter behind a million backs, finally eroded the regime. The communists could suppress the Prague Spring of 1968, could send history professors to stoke boilers, journalists to clean windows, academics to man flower-stalls, but they could not stop the sly subversion of ridicule. Ridicule of the pretensions of an oppressive rule sprang from the character and tradition of the Czech people. It was expressed in the films, plays and novels of the national culture and – by a suitably ironic twist – the lampooned authorities did not seem to notice.

During the 1998 Prague Seminar on evolving European consciousness, it steadily dawned on British participants in the group devoted to culture that defining identity and according the proper role to local and national expressions had become a British as well as a European concern. Almost as much time was spent on the cultural experience of Scotland as on that of Serbia. If this seemed at first odd and was certainly unexpected, the analysis of the 'Scottish Question' was instructive. It went like this. For 250 years after the Union, and culminating in the Thatcher years, Scotland was not only subordinated to England politically but culturally as well. You do not have to be a card-carrying member of the SNP to recognise a certain truth in the perception that Scottish 'culture' had been virtually Leninised – that is to say reduced to a few token, vestigial symbols such as bagpipes, tartan, shortbread, haggis, whisky, a folksy accent and the bacchanalian celebrations of Hogmanay. It is undoubtedly the case that many Scots were happy to collaborate in the process.

No matter that during this same period Glasgow enjoyed a rebirth as 'Glasgow – City of Culture', or that the Glasgow School of painting flowered, the Scottish Colourists were rediscovered and Charles Rennie Mackintosh was re-appreciated. The continuing status granted by England to Scottish national culture was a subordinate, merely cute, one. But as with Czechoslovakia, there was a rebellious strain of an authentic Scottish identity which was alienated from Thatcherite London and later contributed to the sudden sweep towards the idea of self-government, and possibly even independence.

Yet, if Scotland is finding a way out of enforced inferiority and towards a new self-definition, this leaves a new problem of national delineation within Europe: Who are the English? What is Englishness? For years the English have imposed 'Britishness' on the component parts of the United Kingdom. Yet they also inflicted it on themselves. The English were rightly rebuked in no uncertain terms for using 'English' as if it were the most important component of 'Britishness'. For the Scots, Welsh and Irish, it was possible to be a nation and 'British' as well. But the price for their accepting Britishness was only tolerable if the English themselves, and alone within the United Kingdom, turned their back on their own particular national identity. The resulting paradox was that the 'English' could only be 'British'. They have been long bereft of legitimate, respectable ways of reflecting an English identity. The Cross of St George has been captured as an emblem of English nationhood by the least attractive, most violent and chauvinistic parts of the football-hooligan Far-Right. This leaves the task of recapturing ideas and the symbols of Englishness for England as a major task. A nation that has no clear cultural identity will also find the definition of its political nature very hard.

But there is a further lesson for all European cultures, whether they represent the voices of a region or nation, or the greater chorus of the whole European experience. All need to beware of a fake internationalism – that of the commercially branded global multi-nationals whose only interest is to eliminate differences. These seek to produce common products, uniform brands, and a unified corporate culture that springs neither from local experience, political background nor from artistic cross-fertilisation, but solely from the market-analysed reductionism of pecuniary opportunism. You cannot build any sort of identity on such a basis; nor is it intended that you should. For the merchants of this globalisation – who in certain manifestations include the 'harmonising' bureaucrats of Brussels – local diversity is an inconvenient obstacle to the most efficient manufacture and distribution of a series of universal, homogenised products. Their advocates and salesmen peddle a one-taste culture, one-style clothes, one-type organisation. This is not what Europe has created; this is not what Europe needs; this is not a solution for Europe's cultural and political problems.

Yet it is not as easy as that. You cannot saddle the multinationals with all the blame. We their customers must take our share. In the first flush of post-communist nationalism, the outward and visible signs of Western, internationalist consumption were potent and even revolutionary. Jeans, trainers, blousons and burgers marked the transition from Communist-Party-directed orthodoxy to apparent freedom, and above all to freedom of choice in what people bought. (The fact that these consumer goodies were also components of a commercially directed orthodoxy was less important for the time being.) The politics of plenty after a generation of the economics of restriction was heady. The challenge in these countries as they try to catch up with the huge head start of Western European prosperity is whether they can move from the customs of consumption to the culture of creation.

The task for European culture is to admit to itself that rock and pop music, video and advertising culture, trainers and jeans have given post-communist youth a set of cultural symbols more attractive, persuasive and conducive to unity than anything created on the continent in the last two millennia. Eurocrats for their part have to concede that political allegiance to a new undivided land mass has come not through indoctrination into the political and legal values of the institutions of Brussels but to the icons of international consumerism. For both – Europe's culture and its institutions – this is a hard message.

If there is a lesson be learned, it is that Europe needs a hierarchy of cultural identities, founded in regional or local expression, growing into national forms which are increasingly self-confident in their own work and which draw freely and richly from a wide range of international influences. This would represent a position of such strength that Europe's cultures could foster local variety of cultural growths and keep at bay the pseudo-globalising forces that speak of culture and identity but want only the standard and the homogeneous. Then, the burgers and the blousons can take their place as the mere decoration on a fundamentally European cake.

4 Culture, Society, Entertainment – Where is the Space for Art?

A cursory glance at the newspaper headlines proves one thing without a second look: no arts institution is easy to run. It was Ray Gunter, the Minister for Labour in Harold Wilson's 1964 Government, who described his job dealing with unemployment, wages and the trade unions as a 'bed of nails'. Getting off the arts world's spiky bed to confront fundamentals such as the place of art in society is overwhelmingly attractive. The bleared managerial eyes can lift from the computer screen, the mind detach itself from the uncertain horizons of a five-year plan based on annual funding, spreadsheets can be folded away, strategic targets set aside, the setting and fulfilment of objectives put off to a wet day, the congruence of Objectives with the Mission Statement temporarily shelved. From time to time it is useful – no, necessary – to ask the only questions worth addressing. What are the arts for? Where do they take their place alongside society's other preoccupations? We ought occasionally to test the arts against ideas of culture, society and entertainment in order to judge what their standing is and what their role should be.

Of course, we are already in the area of demarcation disputes – more stabs of pain to make Ray Gunter groan. For some people, the arts are coterminous with culture – indeed, a culture without arts could be said to be no sort of culture at all. The arts are an essential, perhaps defining, ingredient of any society worth the name – again, if a society has no culture what kind of society is it? And if the arts do not entertain, as well as all the other things expected of them, their fate will be a sad and speedy one. If this is right, then the very idea of implied contradictions may be bogus.

There are no tidy demarcations here. Are not the overlaps between the categories rather greater than the distinctions?

It is precisely because these terms part company at all that it is a valuable exercise to disentangle them further, to examine them as if they really were separate concepts. This is not just a game. I believe that the differences between culture, society, entertainment and the arts are real and growing larger and that we have to take the signs of this parting of the ways seriously.

To begin with, the perception of culture has become so broad, so inclusive that the word no longer belongs to the arts alone and cannot be monopolised by them. Ideas of society and community have grown more complex and qualified, too. Just as ethnic and social diversity has splintered the old simplicities of the socio-economic class system, so the arts no longer fit clearly into most of the definitions. As for entertainment, well this is the age, the generation of global, mass, instant and perpetual entertainment. That world could – and does – exist without any reference to the arts beyond the occasional act of cultural pillage and exploitation presented as an act of obeisance. (Slap a bit of Dvořak's *New World* symphony onto the bread advert to raise the tone of the commercial break; elevate televised football by prefacing it with Puccini or Fauré; tack Strauss's *Also Sprach Zarathustra* on any project or product where you want a vaguely futuristic feel.)

In short, I hear the sound of tearing of old connections between ideas that were once close, even automatic, partners. If I am right, then there is real cause for concern about the arts and their links with culture, society and entertainment. How long before the arts have to reply to Eliza Doolittle's defiant song of independence from Professor Higgins in *My Fair Lady*: 'I can do bloody well without you!'

Let me start with two personal vignettes. It is a January morning not so long ago and I am reading the papers over breakfast – newsprint as much as marmalade being an essential ingredient of morning digestion. A great many column inches are devoted to a new survey, 'British Lifestyles', on how we live today, what we enjoy, what we spend money on and so on.

Reading about how others spend their money is always fascinating. The survey has a deadly sting in the tail, just the single observation: 'In general the British public has little time for the arts.'

Second vignette. I am browsing through W. H. Smith at Heathrow to see if any half-way-respectable novels catch the eye for airline reading. At one end of the shop, the label 'Lifestyle' heads a whole racked wall of magazines. On closer inspection, every one of them is devoted to some aspect of sex. Now, I do not want to pretend to a naiveté that I do not have, but I had thought that at least some of the lifestyle section might be about something else – motorcars, gardening, clothes, wine, CDs. No, there was just cover after cover of sex and its overwhelmingly laddish indulgence and exploitation.

The second vignette momentarily explained the first. If the British public has little time for art, are they all spending their time indulging in 'lifestyle' between consenting adults? Can things be as bleak as that? Not necessarily. There are other cases of random, anecdotal evidence which point in the opposite direction and to more hopeful conclusions.

Several pieces of news suggest the sheer practical usefulness that the arts have beyond their usual boundaries. A regional rail operator started playing Delius – precise works unspecified – over the loudspeakers on a station's platforms in an attempt to cheer the place up. Lo and behold, the crime rate at that railway station dropped significantly. The mind boggles. Was Delius so soporific that he simply bored vandals out of lawlessness? Is he uniquely the most effective at soothing the savage delinquent breast? Field trials should be held to determine whether other composers restore law and order even more dramatically.

In education, the evidence is stacking up that teaching of the arts produces huge benefits to the whole of the learning process. A research study in 1993 established that listening to Mozart boosted IQ scores in intelligence tests and enhanced students' spatial reasoning performance. Another test demonstrated that taking part in art and drama activities led to significant improvement in the quality, range and imagination of students' writing. One 1997 project showed that pupils who learned the piano performed better in mathematics computation; while another study in the same year found that a positive mood-change among disturbed children was produced by playing them music as part of the daily routine.

A more surprising instance of the power of music came from abroad. Turkish police authorities have attempted to stop their ferocious riot police from being, well, quite so ferocious. As part of their state-of-the-art riot suppression gear, the new helmets contain internal transceivers through which the policemen hear their orders. But they receive more than mere orders. As the troops wait, tense, poised for perhaps bloody confrontation, Mozart and Beethoven will be fed into their minds in order to restrain their violent impulses. The Turkish police authorities must have calculated that Western music inspired by Turkish martial influences – like Mozart's *Rondo alla Turca*, or his *Seraglio* Overture – might be counter-productive, being both nationalist and unduly reminiscent of the warlike tones of the Janissaries' Band. No doubt Beethoven's military set-piece *Wellington's Victory*, where British and French armies clash musically, should be off the police's play-list too. Beyond that, the field is wonderfully open, with Beethoven's *Moonlight* Sonata at the top of the list as likely to slow heartbeats and reduce stress symptoms.

Back home, Sunderland Football Club adopted the march from Prokofiev's *Romeo and Juliet* ballet music as its theme for the team's march onto the pitch at the beginning of the match. The club also programmes classical dance performances with orchestra during the half-time break. The vigour of the Prokofiev march is said to disconcert visiting teams by its assertiveness, far less blatant and purely confrontational than the All Blacks' pre-match 'Hakka', and the football crowd loves the classical ballet.

Not to be left out, another football club has advanced straight into the heartland of arts sponsorship. Entering the Royal Academy in London for the English Regional Art Treasures exhibition in 1997, the sponsors' boards proclaimed that the exhibition's unlikely backers were Peterborough United. Their motto: 'Where Football and Art Meet'. If that slogan has a deliberately unresolved air to it – is Peterborough's football as good as art? Does art feature in the ground and the club? – it offers a teasing mix. Something is going on; some curious, tentative, limited synthesis between art and the rest of culture, a recognition that art is not quite so remote from daily occupations as it is accused of being, something very much more than tarting up commerce with a layer of artistic cosmetic.

None of that, however, solves the problems or removes my anxieties about the threats to the arts. We must return to those tiresome and tricky definitions and distinctions set out at the beginning. As in showjumping, the only way to take a series of difficult jumps is to carry them in one great flowing swing without hesitation.

Thus: 'Culture' includes all the ways in which we think and behave.

'Society' consists of the structures in which our behaviours are regulated and controlled.

'Entertainment' embraces all the ways in which we spend time when we are not working for a living.

The 'Arts' represent all those creative activities which are distinct from the other three but which attempt to make sense and meaning out of them.

If those definitions are correct, then they contain a danger by seeming to push the arts to the periphery; the others can get along perfectly well without them. More, the activities embraced by culture, society and entertainment are now so varied, available and engrossing that the time or inclination to devote time or money to the arts is declining. Has society got other, better, easier things to do?

At first glance, a rich, developed, consumer society such as Britain has never had so many diversions available to it. Leaving aside the desperate experience of enforced unemployment, actual free time, the precious hours not spent working for a basic living, has been transformed into leisure. Leisure has become an industry, and a growth industry at that.

Take home-listening to music. In 1985, only 2% of households had CD players. By 1995, the proportion had risen to 56% and is

still higher today. Over the same period, CD sales have rocketed.
In 1981, a miserable 3.1 million were sold; in 1993, the number
stood at 93 million a year. A break-down of those sales by music
categories reveals that two-thirds of the total were of rock and
pop. Only 7% of CD purchases were of classical music and a mere
2% were of jazz. Contrary to popular assumptions, jazz lovers are
a very select minority, and – numerically at least – not
particularly significant. They are, however, very vocal, very
knowledgeable and very persistent in demanding attention for
their type of music.

Since those figures were compiled, by the middle of 1998 the
classical CD market had taken a further down-turn with its
supposedly 'classical' lists increasingly padded with compilations,
easy listening, mood transformers and pop crossover artists.

The video recorder has also won its place by the hearth. By
1995, 80% of UK households had a VCR but demand for them
was still not satisfied. Sales of VCRs hit a new record in that
year, with no fewer than 25% of homes owning two or more
machines, many of them presumably of the latest model.

What do people use them for? In 1986, the value of the video-
rental market was seven times larger than that for buying videos.
By 1992, the value of bought videos was running neck and neck
with the value of rented ones. By 1995, the video purchase
market was 50% larger than the rental market. At about the
same time, those households that bought videos had on average
26 pre-recorded tapes in their possession. (No doubt most of
those were destined to wither unseen, a reproach and a reminder
of all the good programmes we should have watched!)

What videos did customers buy? In the all-time Top-Twenty
list of bought videos, the top seven are all Disney productions.
The Jungle Book heads the sales list and *Bambi* romps in at
number seven. Not a lot of art there. We should marvel at the
unerring instinct of Walt Disney for creating a well-nigh
universal set of myths of reassurance. Certainly, the demand for
them appears to be virtually limitless. Should we concede
without demur such a tyranny over taste and understanding,
however voluntarily accepted?

CDs and videos are for private home consumption. The home, especially the satellite-driven one, is the most available entertainment centre. But audiences are increasingly going out for their entertainment. While cinema-going will never return to the heady days of the 1960s, its revival in the 1990s and the upswing in British film production have been much noticed and lauded features of the present cultural/artistic scene. Film-making is hailed as one of the 'creative industries' by which the newly rebranded Britain is identified and from which it will flourish. The number of cinema screens doubled in the decade from 1985 to 1996, and annual attendances increased by 45 million or some sixty per cent during the same period. No self-respecting commercial centre or shopping mall is complete without its multiplex, offering a choice of films undreamed of in the post-war heyday of film-going. At that time, peace was the rarity, rationing a normality, every film ran for a week at the local, every programme had a 'B' feature and the idea of choice was an undemanded luxury.

The range of available pastimes does not end there. By the middle of this decade, the number of homes with satellite TV had grown to fourteen per cent of the total; the numbers subscribing to cable systems was rising fast but from a very low base. Yet in the TV viewing world, an interesting phenomenon is discernible. As the number of channels increases overall, as the total amount of viewable material grows exponentially, the total time actually spent in viewing any television falls.

In the three years up to 1995, viewing had fallen by some ten per cent in those homes with access to satellite and cable – that is to say, homes with the highest volume of television material to choose from watched less. What will be the impact of the much-hyped new digital revolution, releasing hundreds of channels onto a public mainly still content with five plus a video recorder? Is the audience really yearning for choice in terms of greatly increased numbers of channels? Or will the digital operators be denied the bonanza they hope for and need? All we know at present is that increased supply does not appear to stimulate demand. The reason may be that quality determines viewing rather than quantity, and no amount of mouthing of the word 'choice' means anything unless it is associated with better programming. There is a warning for the arts there.

Taking all these trends together, there have never been more alternative calls on people's time, leisure and money than there are today. Most are easier to enjoy than the activities offered by the arts. Most are far cheaper, especially satellite television, although even there price is a deterrent to subscription. Most of today's diversions are far more convenient, do not involve a journey, do not demand prior booking and some are available at the flick of a remote control. Most of them set out to entertain as part of their basic assumption. Most of them seek to find out what has pleased the audience in the past and then try to repeat that known success. By contrast, the permanent commitment of the arts to innovate, to challenge, to unsettle, even to disturb, sets them at a distance from the other available diversions. By definition, by choice, by their very nature, they are on something of a loser in today's 'easy-please' social circumstances.

It is not therefore surprising that the statistics for the way we use the arts in all their shapes and forms present a more complex, more confused picture than those for the worlds of entertainment. Some aspects are encouraging. In each year during the decade up to 1994, no less than 25% of the adult population said they had gone to the theatre. This would create a core play-going audience of some 9 million. If that looks momentarily reassuring for the arts, consider the composition of these 9 million theatre visits. Most are to musicals, closely followed by children's plays and the annual, seasonal rite of the pantomime. Remove those three categories and the audience left for classical or contemporary theatre is remarkably small.

Or consider the audiences for live classical music, an activity less popular than going to the cinema or visiting the betting shop. In a recent survey, 33% of respondents said they had been to the cinema in the previous three months; 19% had been to a museum – Sunday afternoon museum-going has replaced the weekly visit to church for many. Just 8% – a low figure, you may think – had been to a pop concert and 7% to a classical concert.

If that 7% appears hearteningly large, further analysis suggested that only two-thirds of that number were truly committed classical music attenders, representing at best a gross number of some $3\frac{1}{4}$ million people. They are certainly a small minority. Yet, according to the Association of British Orchestras, 'there are more people going to concerts! New Halls in Birmingham, Manchester and elsewhere have seen huge surges in audiences, and we have in the BBC Proms the world's best attended and most successful festival of orchestral music.' A true observation so far as it goes, but the financial indebtedness of many British orchestras points to an arts sector with more than its share of problems.

With all statistics, and impressions, interpretation is important. Raw numbers are not to be taken at face value, nor does the single snapshot figure tell the whole story. Look at the longer trends. For instance, the audience for opera has grown by a quarter in the last eight years. It is immeasurably larger than it was fifty years ago when a permanent British opera company, not to mention two national companies and three regional companies, could only have been an opera fanatic's dream. Audiences for ballet and dance have expanded too, given the increased supply and availability of national and international touring companies. As the Association of British Orchestras pointed out, there are more orchestras now than there were fifty years ago; more children studying music; more engagement between musicians and children in schools themselves.

Encouraging as those observations are, it is still impossible to escape the conclusion that – statistically at least – the arts are firmly on society's sidelines. According to 'British Lifestyles', the amount we spend on holidays and entertainment has increased by eleven per cent in the last decade. But once spending on the Lottery, cinema-going, health and fitness clubs and bowling alleys is removed – 'lifestyle' spending if ever there was – most of that increase has been accounted for. The arts do not feature as a prime call on money available for most people's discretionary spending. The evidence from every arts venue is that audiences have to watch their budgets, are very sensitive to price increases,

have eagle eyes for bargain subscription offers, do not wine and
dine regularly or lavishly as part of their evening out, and choose
carefully when and where to spend their hard-earned pounds. For
those with money to spend, the preferred venue for a good night
out is not a concert hall, a theatre or an art gallery. It is a newly-
built, all-purpose, multi-entertainment leisure centre.

Yet before we descend into terminal despair, other, more
cheering, pieces of evidence must be put into the balance. For
instance, in an Arts Council survey, half the public say they
'personally value' having arts events and facilities in their
neighbourhood. A majority agree with the proposition that 'arts
have a beneficial impact on the area they live in'. More than half
say that the arts improve the local quality of life. Just over two-
thirds judge that the arts keep town centres lively and make
them more attractive to visit. These are 'soft', unquantifiable
indicators; they will not sell tickets or fund theatre companies.
Yet they are clear, valuable and positive perceptions.

Nor are they just British perceptions. Recently, the City of
Amsterdam commissioned a study of the social and economic
significance of the professional arts for Amsterdam. It found that
the arts contribute significantly to the regional economy; that
they create jobs; that part of Amsterdam's overall character and
appeal for visitors of all kinds is defined by its arts. The economic
justification is solid.

Yet, the survey's most important findings related to how the
arts make people feel. While 87% said they were 'proud' of
Amsterdam's cultural activities, no fewer than 89% said they 'felt
good' after visiting a given form of art. And 60% said that such
attendance contributed to the development of their knowledge
and taste. Those are very appreciative reactions. Why have the
arts not been able to gain credit for creating this level of approval
and gratitude at the social and personal level? If a national-well-
being index means anything, it should include room for such
indicators.

In the United States, the arts community has delved thoroughly into the reasons for failing to transmit a sense of the value
of the national culture. In Britain, we are too often bogged down

in debilitating anxieties and rows about national and local funding. The Americans have identified explicitly what we acknowledge almost regretfully or apologetically: namely that there is a tussle between private gains and public responsibility, most clearly evident in the world of culture and the arts. Because Americans live in a totally profit-oriented culture, they are far more clear-headed than Britons about the role and value of what they call simply the 'not-for-profit' sector. For the tension between the two sectors can be a creative one.

For Americans of all stripes, the not-for-profit sector is an essential and honourable part of the social environment. In a profit-driven society it is no cause for shame that some activities do not make money. It is recognised as an intrinsic part of their nature. And as a good citizen, it is part of one's civic responsibility to overcome the shortfall as best as one can. Most active American business leaders devote a significant part of their lives and time to working for a 'not-for-profit'. Over there, no one has to apologise for doing so or for actively soliciting support for their pet project; it is expected and recognised as right. Here we are blamed for constantly holding out the begging bowl, because the arts are classed as 'charities', a word with almost irredeemably Victorian overtones of indigence and failure to stand on one's own feet.

Yet even the use of the wholly respectable American category of not-for-profit does not remove all tensions from the country where it was invented. In a major survey of the US arts scene by the National Endowment for the Arts, an American theatre director expressed deep worries that everybody in the British arts world will recognise. 'What all of this debate is about', he observed, 'is driving the not-for-profit culture into the market-place, so that there are no distinctions, so that all of our ideas are shaped by the marketplace. We need enclaves where ideas are not driven by capital, we need not-for-profit enclaves where ideas emerge for other purposes than the advancement of capital.' Those safe havens are concert halls, libraries, museums, galleries, theatres, anywhere that the main activity cannot be quantified, places which flout the increasingly omnipresent orthodoxy that only quantification can truly legitimise anything.

Over the last decade, the arts in Britain have been called on to justify themselves by a whole new series of criteria: they should be efficient and economical; should regenerate the neighbourhood, contribute to employment and wealth creation; should teach by bringing arts into schools and heal by working in hospitals; comfort the elderly, overcome racial disharmony, lower social barriers, alienate no one, cater for the disabled, and meet masses of requirements only recently dreamed up, and by people without knowledge of the arts or experience of them.

The one principle never put at the head of such externally imposed demands is that the art itself should be excellent – creative, innovative and amazing. What a back-to-front set of priorities! Worse, the arts have gained little credit in society's eyes even as they have successfully met the burdensome new objectives laid upon them.

It is no comfort that the Americans have had the identical experience. As one arts centre director complained, though sadly – and typically – in opaque managerial language: 'As we ever more effectively demonstrate our ability to forge synergistic links with diverse and multiple constituencies, often adding considerably to our budgetary commitments, both public and private support for arts institutions is on the decline.' Translated into English: 'As we cope more and more with the external tasks thrust upon us, we get less and less money for our pains from both public and private sources.'

So what must the arts do to earn society's recognition and keep up with the other competitors for our audience's attention? They must be more robust in insisting on management language, terms and prescriptions that are suited to the world of arts. They must harness the new media to their cause. The more CD-ROMs there are about musicians, dancers, writers, painters or museums, the greater the intellectual community of those who share in their irreplaceable and infinitely precious creation. The more the Internet contains information about and knowledge of the arts, the more they will become an essential and inescapable part of its influences and values. Of course, for some people, the screen will be a sufficient point of access to the arts; it will never lead them to a concert or museum. But overall, the CD-ROM will contribute to a greater critical mass of awareness and understanding of the arts than we have now.

In today's world, the arts depend on television and have been deeply damaged by mainstream television's migration from arts coverage as a regular part of television culture. The principal TV stations must show more arts performances and discussions about them on their main channels. The opportunity to use new digital channels as showcases for the best in British live arts creation is a historic one. More operas, concerts, dance and plays – sometimes live, sometimes recorded – would make them routinely accessible. In this way, the arts can reassert their value and become reintegrated into the broader stream of culture as a way of life. Yet the digital route is also a dead end; if the arts are marginalised, turned into a ghetto for the converted, the idea of the arts as a mainstream part of life will never be made. Terrestrial television cannot meet its responsibilities to art by shunting it off into a digital siding.

The arts should hold candid discussions with society in schools, homes, high streets about where and why they part company. They must be honest about facing charges – however unfair they may feel or may be – about being remote, exclusive, irrelevant and incomprehensible. Society must be equally honest in answering charges that it is materialistic, indifferent, superficial and shallow. At the end of such a dialogue, society and the arts may have narrowed the gap between them.

Finally, the arts should rediscover a sense of fun, of light-heartedness, of the joys of diversion. Perhaps there are things to be learned from the sheer professionalism of the worlds of entertainment. I do not believe that the arts singly or collectively live in a Malvolio world where we begrudge anyone the enjoyment of their cakes and ale. Besides the arts should not surrender the vocation of being entertaining so easily to others. They should try to sit more comfortably than they sometimes seem to do with the very idea of entertainment rather than squatting grouchily outside the circus tent.

But equally there are things that the arts must not do. They must never cease to be true to themselves; nor pretend to be easier than they need to be; nor capitulate to anyone who says they are too difficult. They must not be frightened of stating that real rewards require effort from audiences and participants. They should not behave as if they are ashamed of their past or as if their pride in it prevents them from belonging to the future. They must not be coy about what makes them different. Especially in the marketplace of life, they must not sell themselves short.

If they stay true to what they are, but accept the challenge of constructive engagement with their critics, then we could see the arts again interlocked with culture, society and entertainment in a way that satisfies us all.

5 The Good Society – Can You Get It On the Cheap?

It was almost fifty years ago that a group of students at the London School of Economics began to mull over their ideal of what constituted the 'Good Society'. It was a very post-war thing to do. Nazism and Fascism had been defeated. Despite the immediate problems of economic recovery in a European continent devastated by war, things could only get better. True, the Soviet Union was behaving less like the great wartime coalition partner against Hitlerite Germany, more like a state and ideology with its own, alarming agenda. Shouldering these anxieties, it was right for bright, hopeful young men to gather from time to time to think about the grand scheme of things and what could be brighter or grander than contemplating the 'Good Society'?

Forty years later, one member of the 1949 Seminar Group, the philosopher Alan Milne, posed a set of questions relating to the topic and suggested to his friends that they should invite a speaker to try to answer them once a year. John Burgh, one-time Director General of the British Council, subsequently President of Trinity College, Oxford, asked me to do so in 1996. After the customary feeling of regret that I had accepted another speaking engagement, especially one where real thought would be needed, I found that the invitation provided hours of innocent entertainment. It was not only when discussing the subject at home, but on those otherwise duty-led social occasions when a sudden silence was filled by my asking my dinner partner, 'How would you define the Good Society?' It is a well-nigh sure-fire conversation-stopper. The last time I tried it was at the Mansion House. When the look of dismay had left my neighbours' faces, two of them asked nervously how long I had to talk for. 'Ten minutes?' they enquired hopefully. No, I replied, 'more like three-quarters of an hour.' We turned to other, simpler matters.

At first, thinking about what makes a good society appeared attractively simple. All sorts of quick and easy stipulations leaped to mind. Creating a good society brings out the social dictator. For instance: it would be one where all personal counselling was banned on the grounds that it does more harm than good, because it is based on bastard and half-digested Freudianism and because it peddles the fantasy that well-meaning chat, deep 'concern' and a readiness to 'share', without any theoretical foundation to the process, can solve emotional problems.

A good society would have nothing to do with the so-called 'caring' professions. Indeed it would ban them. In their place, it would have the 'indifferent professions', that is to say those organisations who do good because it is their job to help and not because they confuse indulgence in mushy emotions with a professional task. I use the word 'indifferent' as in the translation of the instruction in the lavatories of old French railway trains: 'turn the tap indifferently to left or to right'. The tap works – but not because it cares either way. So would the 'indifferent' professions.

A good society would be one where eating while walking in the street – not to mention throwing away the container – would be banned on the grounds that it is fattening, polluting, and disgusting to look at. Casual eating is no better than casual sex. It damages social cohesion by reducing those occasions when people sit down, face to face, and enjoy a conversation. It trivialises the sacramental experience of breaking bread together. Banning promiscuous, impulse eating in public would help to increase the times that families talked and related to one another – or even learned to sulk in a sociable way – as a group.

A good society might consider banning TV zap-buttons on the grounds that they destroy the ability to concentrate and eliminate any possibility of viewers being stretched or surprised by a programme that catches them unawares before they have the time or energy to get off their couches and change the set manually. Or it might regulate 'flying Australian winemakers', on the grounds that replanting the world's marginal vineyards with millions of hectares of Chardonnay and flinging the result into oak barrels make the resulting vintage taste like toffee and flood the world with hectolitres of wine muzak. Or — well my list, like Gilbert's Lord High Executioner's, would be endless, and continuously updated.

But this was only a personal game. A truly good society could not be based on the impulses and prejudices of the individual, however satisfying that game might be. It certainly should not be founded on bans — hard cases make bad law and even worse social morality. It should offer general principles to which the majority can subscribe because more people will benefit than suffer from the results. Its laws and regulations would not be concerned with stopping people from doing things — the bad society is already far too adept at that — but with encouraging people to do things that are more attractive than the things we are tempted to stop.

But first, let me start with the questions that Alan Milne posed to get the lecture series started in the '90s. How do his own assumptions about a good society stand today, and how well or badly does contemporary Britain fare against them? He called for a society without gender or racial discrimination. With women still experiencing prejudice and unequal opportunities in the job market and with racial attacks in Britain running at the rate of tens of thousands each year, we can hardly feel that we have met his performance target. Yet we have surely moved to a 'Better' if not yet a 'Good' society. Thanks to equal opportunities policies at work and the Race Relations Act (however patchily they are implemented), those discriminated against now have some chance of redress and the more obnoxious forms of bigotry have been labelled as crimes. Is it too much to believe that institutional and legal restraints on behaviour are gradually, if painfully slowly, encouraging changes in perception and that good behaviour will finally drive out bad?

Alan Milne again: 'A good society cannot be indifferent to the plight of the poor, the unfortunate and the helpless in its midst.'

With an underclass of some ten per cent of the population; with more beggars and people sleeping rough in our cities; with hardly a street corner without its seller of the *Big Issue*; with the human experiments of so-called 'Care in the Community' wandering in a bemused way around the nation's streets; with clear proof that increased wealth at the top does not trickle down to the poor below, and the gap between rich and poor growing steadily, our society gives a passable imitation of indifference to the poor and helpless. If there is a social welfare safety net, then its holes seem to be getting ever bigger. We seem to have become deaf to the sounds of bodies falling through that net.

Finally, I can only quote with admiring sadness the sheer idealism of Alan Milne's final sentence: 'If all are to enjoy modest prosperity, some will have to forego part of the greater prosperity they could otherwise have achieved.' *Sancta simplicitas*. It is now part of bipartisan economic and political orthodoxy that the middle and upper classes should not be taxed more highly than they are, that receiving an income of £100,000 a year is not to be considered rich, that enterprise culture demands an enterprise class whose rewards should be limitless and comparable with the greatest available anywhere on earth. In the early years of Thatcherism, a top tax rate of fifty per cent was regarded as perfectly acceptable, generous even. Today, under a New Labour government, the suggestion that this tax rate might be restored is held up as punitive on a Stafford Crippsian scale. If the pips are to be made to squeak, today's squeaking pips belong to the already poor. Who cares about modest prosperity for all? Outstanding riches for some seems a more accurate description of the society we have created. We have a long way to go to meet the criteria sketched out in this very decade for the lecture series.

Ideas for ways to take up the subject came at odd times and odd places. One night, we were reeling out of Covent Garden after *Das Rheingold*. There was John Burgh observing challengingly 'How about that as a theme for the "Good Society"?'

It certainly offers many instructive variations on the theme. Wotan builds Valhalla as a home for the gods and as a sign that he is ending the compulsive globe-trotting and philandering that so annoy his wife, Fricka. He is not the first or the last man to build an ideal home for his wife out of sexual guilt, but he remains as an awful warning to those who contemplate it. Like many conscience-stricken men, he does not have the money to pay for his guilt-nest. Wotan then makes two mistakes. First he mortgages a member of his family – Freia – to the builders. Then, knowing that he will forfeit his mortgage because he does not have the cash to repay it, he employs a shifty spiv called Loge to steal what is necessary to avoid the repo men, the giants Fafner and Fasolt, taking the property they have built. Of course, Alberich and Mime are loathsome dwarves who themselves want to dominate the world, but does that justify stealing the Rheingold from them by lying and trickery?

In all this, Wagner's sense of moral right and wrong is impeccable. His entire cycle is built on the proposition that those who choose absolute power will forfeit the possibility of love. The search for power, once tasted, becomes unquenchable and obsessive, leading to treachery, murder and death. Love can overcome the lust for power but only if it renounces and rejects power, as Brunnhilde does. For reasons unstated, only the Rhinemaidens can handle the source of all power without contamination. But, as the lustful Alberich complains, being slippery as eels perhaps they have no time or inclination or capacity for love as we know it.

Wagner, too, insists on the importance of legality. Wotan, that clear-eyed, but one-eyed god, tries to impose order on the world through a series of treaties and contracts, all recorded and inscribed on the ash staff that he carries with him. But Wotan betrays his own beliefs. 'The trouble with you,' says Fricka, 'is that you don't stick to what you swear to.' Later, the dwarf, Alberich, asserts that Wotan is actually no better than he himself – a practitioner of Realpolitik, all too ready to break his word when it suits his ends.

In short, and nothing else about *The Ring* is short, Wagner presents a moral universe where power corrupts, love conquers, would-be universal rulers are destroyed by the contradictions involved in achieving their ambition, treaties are better kept than broken, and even the supposed hero is sufficiently gullible as to allow himself to be drugged and then to seduce his bride on behalf of someone else. No wonder they all come to a very wet and sticky end. And don't forget the first and also the final lesson: always pay your builders.

On reflection, I first thought about the good society at school, or rather a close and far cleverer friend did the thinking for me. A year older than I was, he kindly allowed me to sit at his feet as he put the world to rights. It was, he asserted, wrong that we young would have to live our mature lives in a world that had been shaped by decisions taken by the old. We were prevented from being responsible for our destinies. Those politicians or so-called statesmen who formed that world for us would not experience the consequences of their actions, for they would be long dead. Everyone should accept responsibility for making the beds of life on which they would have to lie.

'So, Socrates,' I dutifully put in when I could, 'how do we put right this unjust state of affairs?' Socrates obliged. If we were all to learn the moral principle that we must live with the consequences of our own actions, then the government of affairs in a country should be entrusted only to those between the ages of twenty-five and forty. Once we reached forty, we would be disqualified from government, and turn our attention to other matters – learning, the arts, religion, business, commerce or whatever took our fancy.

To objections that the young lacked the experience to govern wisely and well, the sage replied briskly that their abilities had never been tested, whereas if you wanted a monument to the achievements of the old you only had to look at the mess around you. He pushed his argument further: if there were indeed evidence that age and experience produced better government, the reward of learning early about responsibility and living with the consequences of one's actions would still be infinitely preferable.

There, amid the intellectual teasing, my precocious school friend hit on a serious truth: that we should all understand the connection between our acts and their outcomes and be accountable for them. These are crucial ingredients for making mature individuals as well as a good society. In the 1930s, the café entertainer Ronald Frankau, not renowned primarily as a moralist, had a song for it:

> You've got to pay for everything you get.
> It's a matter of considerable regret.
> Needless to repeat it,
> You can't have your cake and eat it,
> Sooner or later you'll have to pay the debt.

From the 1960s onwards, we elevated the business and language of rights above that of responsibilities. From human rights to women's rights, to children's rights to animal rights, the catalogue lengthened and became more sophisticated. It followed inexorably that rights – which were mere abstract aspirations without some weight behind them – required bolstering by being connected to entitlements, usually financial. Thirty years on, it is far from clear that the doctrines of rights have significantly advanced the cause of many of the championed categories, and it is abundantly clear that societies are reluctant or unable to pay the entitlements needed to turn claims into gains. Is it better or worse to deny rights by resisting them, to proclaim rights and then fail to realise them in practice, or to seek to gain a general advance through rights for all rather than pursue particular rights for special groups?

Recently, the public debate has shifted from rights to the seemingly more old-fashioned language of responsibilities. I do not believe that it is old-fashioned in the pejorative sense, but the way it is deployed sometimes has a backward-sounding ring to it. From errant fathers pursued by the Child Support Agency, to indifferent parents required to enter into a contract with their children's school, obligations will be codified, formalised and legalised. You will be told ('counselled' perhaps) how to be a good parent, a good single-parent, a good wife- or husband-to-be, a good ex-husband, and each life stage will have its own code of conduct, even its own charter. But will this new single-minded emphasis on responsibilities rather than rights achieve in its turn what is hoped for?

Some years ago, when Professor Charles Goodhart – now at the London School of Economics and a member of the powerful Bank of England Economic Monetary Policy Committee – was at the Bank of England, he coined a useful but inadequately noticed maxim. In the field of economic management, he observed, if a single economic indicator was elevated above others as the principal yardstick of the economy's performance, it usually became distorted and ultimately distorted the performance of the economy itself. A similar observation might apply to principles governing social and moral behaviour: to elevate rights alone, or to concentrate purely on responsibilities, invariably leads to imbalance or malformation. They cannot exist by themselves. Treating them in isolation warps the other factors with which they need to interact to make up a good society.

At Cambridge, I was taught medieval history by a great Austrian historian, Walter Ullmann. A lawyer by training, Ullmann applied the study of legal principles and terminology to the workings of the medieval Papacy. He seasoned his lectures with slightly puzzled, but always pointed, recollections of his time in the British Pioneer Corps during the war. Peopled as it was by politically 'unreliable' exiles such as Walter, the Pioneer Corps must have had the highest average IQ of any British military unit. One day, as the Sergeant Major ran his recruits ragged across the parade ground, Ullmann found himself reflecting on the institution to which he now belonged. Could it really be, as it seemed, one in which a few had unlimited powers and the majority, like himself, had none? Or was it not, surely, like a Roman 'corporatio'? If the latter, then any member must have duties, rights and privileges.

The Sergeant Major dismissed the parade – giving rise to another Ullmannism: 'You know, that is just like the priest who says at the end of the Mass, "Ite, missa est" ' – and Walter decided to make formal enquiries about the true nature of the army from the Company office. He marched in and asked where – since he knew all too much about his army duties – he should look for his rights and privileges. The Duty Corporal marched him back to his barracks so fast that his feet hardly touched the ground.

But Ullmann was right. Duties, rights and privileges are the essential legs of a moral, legal and political tripod. Putting all the weight on one to the exclusion of the others leads to bad laws, bad social practices and buckles the workings of society; omitting one causes it to topple over. Perhaps it is the very swing from rights to duties that causes the instability. Privileges, too, have to be earned, not assumed as a right in themselves. Privileges only accrue when rights and duties have established their own balance.

In Siegfried Lenz's 1960s novel *The German Lesson*, a young man sentenced to prison for stealing paintings is required by his remedial prison regime to look back at his upbringing and the family influences that might have led him to jail. He remembers the deep sense of duty by which his father, a local policeman in Germany in the 1930s and 1940s, worked. When the Ministry of Culture in Berlin ordered that a local artist (clearly based on the Expressionist Emil Nolde) should be banned from painting, the dutiful policeman not only delivered the instructions but zealously enforced them, ensuring the painter was punished when they were ignored, even though the man had been his friend since childhood. A compulsive sense of duty, of properly executing his official responsibilities, carried all before it, unmediated by any sense that in doing right by himself and by his office, he might be denying the rights of another human being. In this caricature of responsibility — better presented as blind obedience — the policeman was untroubled by conflict between responsibility to the state and the claims of old friendship.

The rebellious policeman's son, however, had his own sense of duty. It impelled him to protect the artist's paintings from destruction by his father by removing them. Was he preserving or stealing them? But even this initially defensible moral drive itself became distorted as the young man began to take anyone's pictures when he had mere premonitions that they might come under threat.

Society, a good society, cannot be constructed on the basis of a single criterion, a social variant on the kind of 'one-club economics' for which Chancellors of the Exchequer were often excoriated. Here too the choices before us are polarised as lying between the market and the community. (We were assured, of course, under Thatcherism that 'society does not exist'! Blairism has reinstated it.) For many years, the model of the free market has been held up as the unchallengeable, indeed moral, foundation on which a good society should be based. Markets allow freedom, swap information, generate innovation, stimulate economic activity, allow competition, motivate enterprise and are the best form of social activity devised by man.

Yet markets – real or theoretical – are not filled with plaster saints whose main aim is to meet the public's demands for the most innovative goods and the most reliable services at the lowest possible price. Markets are filled with people who want to corner them, with hucksters, con-men and opportunists. The traders talk loudly about choice as if choice alone was an unchallengeable moral good. As Adam Smith – but not the Adam Smith Institute – observed, the natural impulse of any group of businessmen when they gather together is to exploit the market to their benefit as much as to pour benefits on their customers. From Gordon Gekko to Michael Milken to Ivan Boesky to John Meriwether, the financial free market's 'Lords of the Universe' have behaved – and been taken at their own valuation – as if they had built the machine that made gold. Ben Jonson would have loved it.

The language of the market has now to influence, even to dominate, most human activities. Any organisation worth its salt is supposed to exist by an internal market – though the National Health Service is now recognised as being unsuitable for it. This means that each and any transaction must be costed and can only occur if a price is put upon it; this price must be the lowest available. Purist advocates of the system would rather the transaction was costed in theory and not used than that it should take place on an imperfect cost basis. Not knowing the price of a transaction is now the ultimate managerial – human, even –

crime. To those who say that any transaction is only justifiable if its cost is known, I offer the words of the prayer: 'To give and not to count the cost'! The most cherishable human transactions in a good society are precisely those that are not costed because those concerned believe that the spirit of such uncalculated giving is essential to making a good society work.

But even within the narrower confines of an organisation, to turn relationships into market transactions, to put a price on them, is to miss the point. It reduces co-operation between individuals and creates administrative and bureaucratic barriers; it sets a price on ideas; it destroys a sense of corporate community; it fragments a sense of corporate belonging; it dehumanises because it materialises the human traffic of feelings, of curiosity, the satisfactions of mutual working together.

There is a graphic example of this tendency from the BBC World Service. While I was Managing Director, consultants urged us to price the use of the Library and Information service on the grounds that it was costing a lot of money to run. Some members of staff, it was alleged, used it too much. What, I asked, did 'using it too much' mean? The answer was that some staff used it more than the average. Perhaps, I objected, that reflected their diligence, their professionalism, their dedication, their concern to maintain standards. Perhaps they should be encouraged to use it still more. Possibly, came the reply, but the Library and Information centre could be run more cheaply if fewer people used it. I retorted that since the whole standing and credibility of the World Service rested on its accuracy, what was the point of saving a few pounds on a central service if you then risked losing the only priceless asset the organisation possessed – its reputation? Such are the purblind lengths to which the disciples of cheapness are ready to go. It is the modern *trahison des clercs*.

Management consultants know that the really worthwhile activities cannot be priced; but because they are unwilling or unable to confer a value on them, they try to imprison them within the confines of a price bracket or deny their validity at all. You cannot have a newspaper or a World Service that is accurate

ninety per cent of the time. Almost anything that it costs to
deliver the final ten per cent of accuracy or excellence is not just
good value for money but an essential expenditure without
which all prior costs would be a waste of time and money. The
last ten per cent of expenditure may well create the real value,
the one that defies analysis.

Yet the pressure of such a reductive outlook is relentless. How
cheaply can a service be provided? That has become the ultimate
question of existence, the principal justification of any activity.
In the land of the cost-driven, the lowest tenderer is king. Only
later do you discover the real bases on which the tender was
submitted and realise that many a cost reduction has a service
reduction built into it. A good society would balance the current
obsession with price by an added concern for quality. That would
indeed add value to the process of buying the best products,
accepting the best contracts, supplying the best services. If value
is intrinsically unmeasurable, it is also simply priceless. Were all
the acts and goods supplied by individuals and enlightened
institutions for non-economic reasons to be costed out, they
would represent an industry of billions of pounds whose true
contribution to society would still remain incalculable.

I have no doubt that some management consultant would
establish that trying to cost the uncostable involved a vast waste
of public resources and should be adequately prioritised or
stopped altogether. Alternatively, that such an activity was so
economically important that it should immediately be scrutinised
for value for money. Surely the Good Samaritan would have
been well advised not to tarry by the wayside (even though Mrs
Thatcher thought he could help because he could afford to). He
should have stopped to calculate the opportunity cost of the time
he might spend in helping the man set upon by thieves. He
might decide that it was economically more efficient to hurry by
on the other side, despatching a team of consultants to persuade
the battered man of the dangers of becoming dependent on
others.

Beyond threatening a sense of the truly valuable, the
untrammelled market damages notions of a good society by

challenging the very concept of the individual. In such forms of market differentiation, old-fashioned class and social background are replaced by categories such as 'Stylish Singles', 'Pebble-dash Subtopians', 'Rootless Renters', or 'Bijou Homemakers'. Such 'geo-demographic segmentation' is an essential marketing tool for anyone engaged in the business of selling. The titles may be facetious, but their purpose is serious: to sub-divide individuals into minute selling units, niches to be targeted in and by the market. No one would answer to being a member of the 'Suburban Mock Tudor' category, still less to being a denizen of the 'Bulldog Estates', though honesty might demand recognising oneself as 'Ageing Professional', 'Moneyed Emigré', or 'High-spending Grey'. In days gone by, all those would have fitted snugly and happily into a different sub-group: 'Corporate Careerists'. Whichever title is given, in the world of the market everyone fits into a category, and a sub-category of a sub-category. Abandon any thought of being an individual defined by personality and belief, with aspirations to breadth of understanding, willingness to experiment.

In the world of the market you are fixed by age, education, income and a few expressed tastes into one category and no other. You no longer inhabit a society in common with other individuals. The market is not interested in what binds us together. It wants to know only how small and particular is the group into which we can reliably be corralled. It has a vision of a world of niches, where each one is separated from, wholly indifferent to, perhaps even hostile to, the values, wishes and interests of those in other niches. It thrives by fragmentation, by differentiation, through exclusivity rather than inclusivity, through disintegration rather than integration. It is a kind of marketplace apartheid. The citizen has ceased to exist, to be replaced by the target group. The market is not interested in who you are or what you believe, only what you will buy.

Set against this, a good society should offer a concept of citizenship which relates to others, which sees people in the round, and which adds what they have in common to what they are entitled to have for themselves. The market works in the opposite direction, leading to a balkanisation of identity, the elevation of the consumer, the purchaser, the customer over the broader, more humane categories of citizen, individual, member of the public, member of the family, part of the audience. A good society cannot be based on a rainbow coalition of minority rights or tastes; the more it is founded on such particularities, the less it will be founded on an inclusive sense of rights and duties open to all.

The members of the student group who began musing over the big issues of life fifty years ago have many of the ingredients of a good society. They meet because they like one another, because they value ideas, continuity, human exchange, and they do not set a cost on the activity. Their personal transactions are those of friendship. Where is friendship today? Not in the marketplace. Not in cyberspace. But then fraternity has always been the weak link in the holy Republican triumvirate.

A good society does not confuse ecstasy with enlightenment; it does not confuse atomisation with individuality; price and cost with value; exploitation with enterprise; reward with greed; cornucopia with choice; abundance with riches; elitism with exclusiveness; organisation with effectiveness; structures with relationships; noise with meaning.

The Mexican philosopher Ivan Illich was right to emphasise the importance of conviviality as a crucial social value. Unless some social activity, some urban project, some new institution contributed to an increase in human conviviality, then it was useless. As a single criterion for testing whether a policy or a decision advances the arrival of the good society, it cannot be bettered.

Part Two: Politics

6 I'm Worried About Tony*

Some readers will remember the familiar complaint of the eponymous writer of *Mrs Dale's Diary*, mother of all radio soaps. 'I'm worried about Jim,' she would confide anxiously, Jim being her doctor husband. Well, I am worried about the Prime Minister and the curious ideas he seems to have about the arts world; not just his ideas, but some significant blank spots in his view of them. Both – ideas and blank spots – account for the government's failure to treat the arts properly or sensibly. I am not the only one who is 'worried about Tony'. The Culture Department is worried sick too.

Let's start with those parties at Number 10. By all means invite the 'celebrity' world, the rock and pop world, the showbiz world, to bask in New Labour sunshine once. (Though judging by Damon Albarn's dismissal of the parties as 'disgusting and vulgar', perhaps a comment on Noel Gallagher, not all were impressed.) But to do so three times and to overlook the world of arts so thoroughly is pretty alarming.

Does Tony Blair really enjoy talking to Noel Gallagher more than he might, say, to John Tomlinson, the greatest Wagnerian bass in the world? Does he really enjoy chatting to Chris Evans or to Zoë Ball more than he might to, say, Beryl Bainbridge, Ian McEwan or Martin Amis? He could have invited fewer pop-group representatives and added a classical group such as the Lindsays, one of Britain's finest string quartets, or discovered the sprightly diversity of the Nash Ensemble players. He could have asked Dame Judi Dench or Juliet Stevenson, as well as Liz Dawn

* This article appeared in *The Times* on 11 March 1998.

of *Coronation Street*. As it was, they were very lop-sided lists, doing no sort of credit to Britain's internationally acclaimed arts achievers.

So, I'm worried about the Prime Minister because he is signalling that Oasis is as important to Britain as opera; that chat shows are as important as novels; that television soap-operas are more valuable than live theatre; and that all sorts of other key ingredients of the arts matter not at all. If it had happened just once, then it would not have been worth mentioning, but three times – not to speak of the official heavyweight Cabinet turnout at the Britpop awards (did all those ministers really want to be there?) – is no accident, comrades.

But there is worse to come. It is quite clear that the Prime Minister simply does not understand why the arts world is in such an uproar at New Labour's funding failures in the arts field. He is puzzled and has asked the Culture Ministry – more in anger than in sorrow – what is going on?

The puzzlement is said to stem from his conversion to the idea of the 'Creative Industries'. For in New Labour ideology, only the 'Creative Industries' count and the Government has been assiduous in devising policies directed to helping them. Given that, everything should be rosy. But the Prime Minister fails to understand that the 'Creative Industries' – film, video, TV, design, rock and pop – essential and admirable as they are, are only a part of the world of the arts, in some cases an applied extension of them. Having bought the idea of their importance and of the need to support them, he stopped looking beyond their boundaries.

In backing 'the arts that pay', and overlooking and undervaluing 'the arts that cost', Mr Blair shows himself to be the true son of Margaret Thatcher. In New Labour's Victorian world where the virtuous work and earn, the arts may (claim to) work but they manifestly do not earn – they are a cost to the community, a charge to the taxpayer, a burden on the citizen. This makes them less desirable – to New Labour – and certainly less deserving, than the virtuous worlds of the 'Creative Industries'. So their indigent representatives do not cross the portals of Downing Street.

But the confusion about where the arts start – or finish – and the creative industries begin goes deeper still. 'New Labour' was a triumphant exercise in re-branding – new people, new title, new logo, new colour, new clothes, new language – and now 'New Britain' has to be re-branded too. Out goes anything to do with the past, out goes anything to do with culture or continuity because it has been branded as – the killer word – 'heritage', and somebody has persuaded Mr Blair – or perhaps he needed no persuading – that the arts are just dead heritage; backward-looking, stuffy, uncreative and unsellable to foreigners.

Leave aside the fact that a casual glance at the arts scene in Britain – whether theatre, literature, dance, music or painting – will show them to be exploratory and innovative as well as aware of their historical roots, the h-word – a Reaganite formulation in any case, destructively adopted by the Thatcherites – has been foisted onto the arts and now hangs around their collective neck like the proverbial albatross. But it has been pinned on the arts by outsiders and is no part of the way the arts see or describe themselves. As a result of the pejorative use of the h-word, the arts are not only not included in the grand project of the re-branding or projecting of New Britain, they must be seen to be excluded in a very public way.

And one further bogey word has now been pinned onto the arts – 'elite'. I'm worried that Mr Blair is terrified of being caught even looking elitist. I know that Prime Ministerial Diaries are very full, but he does get to the theatre from time to time – he was at the Barbican only last week. Surely he could see for himself how ludicrously inaccurate is the smear of the alleged elitism or exclusivity of the arts audiences.

And this leads me to the core of my 'worries about Tony'. Simply, that the arts do not matter to him personally because they are a marginal and thinly-rooted side of his own experiences. He is a true child of the sixties; the rock and pop world is the one that he likes instinctively; he is simply not at ease in the arts world. His evident lack of esteem for it – as evidenced by the way his government treats it – springs from that essential personal discomfort.

Now, I may be wrong. I hope I am. But all his actions signal the reverse: that he has pop stars to his parties because he feels most comfortable with them. By contrast, the arts are now lumbered in the Prime Minister's mind with a heap of pejorative associations. We can expect little sympathy, minimal under-standing, and feeble support for the financial crisis in which the performing arts now find themselves. Against this damaging, personal, Prime Ministerial mindset, weak protestations from the Culture Ministry count for nothing. That's why 'I'm worried about Tony'.

7 What Happened at Downing Street

A short time after I had voiced my 'worries about Tony' in *The Times*, the Prime Minister came to the Barbican to open a business conference on the need to take the Millennium Bug seriously. As is usual on these occasions, I was asked to meet and greet him. It was too good a chance to miss for pinning his ear back on the subject of the arts. It was 30 March 1998.

Neither he nor his staff – who were out in full force – made any reference to the article, barbed or otherwise. But after his speech, and a photocall in our foyer with the Covent Garden Soup Company – chosen because they were regarded as exemplary in their planning to mitigate the effects of the Millennium Bug – I escorted Tony Blair out of the building.

'Prime Minister, I would very much like the opportunity to come and talk to you about the arts. I realise you are frantically busy but I would value half an hour of your time at some stage.'

'We're not getting the arts right?' he queried as we strode along to the back-stage lift. 'Is it just about money?'

'It is about money,' I replied, 'but not just money. It is about the government's attitude to the arts as well. There is a perception problem.'

He replied politely that it would, of course, be helpful to have a chat some time. We left it at that.

On 14 April, I decided to take things further and wrote to the Prime Minister to see if I could prod him towards a meeting, supposing that he was inclined to be prodded. Within a fortnight, I got back a letter saying that he was going to hold a seminar on the arts at Number 10 and that the staff would

contact me with details in due course. That due course came
towards the end of May, with an invitation for 29 June 'to get
across some of your ideas, hopes and fears about how Government policy should develop.' Soon after, invited participants to
the seminar were asked to have individual, informal meetings
with two Downing Street staffers – one a civil servant, the other
a political adviser – about preparing the agenda in the light of
the issues we thought important to raise.

Over the next few weeks, the preparatory staff work put into
the seminar was detailed and impressive. Each participant was
seen by the civil servants and each contribution was condensed
into a series of agreed subject headings that covered the topics
that seemed common to most.

In the meantime, I took the opportunity to consult some of my
closest artistic colleagues and partners, such as the London
Symphony Orchestra and the Royal Shakespeare Company, to
make sure that I was representing their views accurately and as
fully as possible. Their comments boiled down to four areas of
concern. First, money. All of them said the resources lost as a
result of four years' cash standstill without an uplift for inflation
had to be restored. This loss was, after all, the main cause of the
arts funding problem. (Later, Richard Eyre in his Report
confirmed that there was an exact match between the accumulated deficits of most organisations and the impact of the
standstill funding. The deficits did not reflect bad management so
much as sustained underfunding.) If after having their core
funding restored these arts bodies received an annual uplift for
inflation – meaning they received no more, but no less in real
terms – and a three-year settlement on this basis, then they could
survive. It would not be riches. It would not be more money in
real terms, but it would mean an end to cuts.

Second, my colleagues expressed deep concern about the
subject I had raised in my *Times* article: the apparent dichotomy
in the government's mind between the so-called 'creative
industries' and the arts. 'In reality,' said one friend, 'they are one.
But the government has put a knife between them.'

Third, there was the deepest anguish about the Lottery. Of

course, it had put millions into capital funding that would not have been available otherwise – to put it in industrial terms, this was money for plant, not for productions or wages. But in the mind of the public, 'the arts are getting millions from the Lottery and they are still moaning.' Collectively, ministers and arts leaders had made a miserable job of telling the public what Lottery money was for and what it was not for. The impression given – and not contradicted – was that the arts world had arbitrarily grabbed a large sum of the 'People's Lottery cash' and was complaining that it was not greater than it was. The fact that it was Parliament which had decided the apportionment of the Lottery money was ineffectually stated and inadequately emphasised.

When, too, the Arts Council had tried to divert some Lottery cash into actual arts activity by devising the 'Arts for Everyone' programme (one heavily inclined to educational schemes that broadened the base of those who could enjoy the arts), the experience of A4E, as it was called, had turned into a ruinous bureaucratic nightmare. The volume and value of applications wildly outstripped the sums of money dedicated to A4E; the Council's officers were drowned in the flood. When the overwhelming majority of applicants were rejected, the bitterness felt at the hours of scarce time, energy, human and other resources wasted in submitting proposals doomed not to be taken seriously was huge. In this context, anger about diversion of money from the arts to the management consultants who either drew up the schemes or evaluated them – using up some twelve to fifteen per cent of the total value of grants given, according to one of my colleagues – was profound and strongly held.

To these common complaints, I identified a further anxiety: even when money was granted, so many strings, forms and conditions were attached that it was far less useful than a single increase in unrestricted funding would be. The danger was that a single grant to an arts institution would now only be supplemented by a series of discrete additional grants – for, say, education, access, outreach – each of which would be subject to individual scrutiny as to its effectiveness in delivering the performance targets devised for it. Apart from increasing the amount of bureaucratic supervision involved, such a process denied any particular arts institution the opportunity to spend the total grant as it thought appropriate, bearing in mind the agreed overall aims of that institution.

Finally, as I talked more widely with friends throughout the arts, there was the matter of the Dome. 'The arts are short of money,' said one friend, 'but the Dome never is. It is a monster. The government has lost credibility with it.' Yet almost everyone felt that even to raise the matter at Downing Street would be counter-productive in view of the government's total commitment to it as a flagship project of its first term in office. Still the sense of outrage about the money spent on the Dome is almost impossible to overstate. Not long ago, I asked one of Britain's greatest pianists what he would say to Tony Blair if he met him. 'First, I would say that I voted for you and I did so because I thought that Britain badly needed a change of direction. Second, that I am now very disillusioned by the way the arts have been treated and by the lack of importance the government gives to them. Then, I would tell him that at a time when the arts are struggling to make ends meet, the sums of money spent on the Dome are just shocking.'

A few days before the seminar, Dennis Stevenson, the outgoing Chairman of the Tate Gallery, who had been named as the chairman of the assembled group of twenty arts worthies, rang us all up, checked that we would have the opportunity to say what we wanted within the agreed format, and invited us to add anything as the discussion took place. He had divided the seminar into five areas for discussion, to give it a focus without stifling debate. The main topics identified in the pre-seminar briefings were listed as: financing the arts; reform, change and management; education; access; and institutions and their inter-relationships.

Dennis's final message was this: 'Don't go on too much; keep to two minutes or less for your first statement. And a bottle of champagne for anyone who keeps a subsequent intervention to less than a minute.' (I do not know who, if anyone, won it.)

For all that twenty leading arts figures were going to talk about
a world publicly identified as being in a state of crisis, the media
got no advance wind of it. This speaks volumes for the discretion
of those involved, but then they were all serious players. They
included Ruth McKenzie, Director of Scottish Opera, Trevor
Phillips, Chairman of the London Arts Board, Sir Simon Rattle,
Genista McIntosh, Managing Director of the Royal National
Theatre, Neil McGregor, Director of the National Gallery, Neil
Cossons of the Science Museum, Melvyn Bragg, and others of a
similar standing. Given the participants, had news of the event
broken over the preceding weekend, the advance speculation
and inevitable position-taking would have made sensible discussion difficult if not impossible. You can imagine the tabloid
headlines – 'Labour in Luvvie Love-In' and such like – that
would have prejudged the tone of the debate and any decisions
reached. As it was, the outward calm and lack of hype served to
make the occasion and the atmosphere constructive.

We were called for 3 p.m. on 29 June on a warm summerish
afternoon, that comparative rarity in the summer of 1998. After
twenty minutes in the Downing Street antechamber with a cup
of tea, Tony Blair, Chris Smith, Geoffrey Robinson (then
Paymaster General at the Treasury), and the Downing Street
staffers appeared. My hunch from the beginning was that the
door was already open to the possibility of an increase in arts
funding. Holding the seminar at all was clear recognition of a
need to put things right or at least righter. Whatever outsiders
might think of the arts leaders assembled, to have called them in
to Downing Street, listened and then to have given the arts
nothing would have been a more obviously calculated rejection
of the arts as a whole than all those Number 10 drinks for rock
stars and pop presenters. Such a slap in the face was unlikely but,
if my guess was wrong, mere tea and sympathy might be all we
got. Whatever the underlying anxieties, the atmosphere in the
Cabinet Room was relaxed, non-confrontational and open in
every sense.

For a start, there was a refreshing readiness to concede fault on
both sides: on the government's that there had been insufficient

dialogue with the arts world; on our side, that arts funding administration had been 'something of a shambles', and that it had to be straightened out rather quickly. The ghost of the Royal Opera hung balefully over the proceedings but, like the Dome, it was a subject put to one side as something that would muddy the overall argument not clarify it.

I was struck, too, how ready the arts side was to admit past weakness in giving grants. There was a whiff of Admiral Byng in the air. If arts funding bodies were to recover public credibility as rigorous dispensers of public money, then some recipients would have to be taken out and shot, '*pour encourager les autres*'. The Greenwich Theatre would not be the last institution to receive this treatment. If factories closed, then why not theatres or orchestras? The arts world must take decisions, said one leading administrator, justify those decisions and then stick to them. Too often, said another, a hard decision to cut support for an institution was taken but was then undone because of 'blind-side' lobbying. If the arts were to be seen to run themselves seriously, such openness to lobbying had to be stopped.

As the ninety-minute meeting wore on, it seemed to me that what we were doing was to put on the table, unconsciously at first, the elements of a new compact. The representatives of the arts were present not merely as penitents or supplicants. They were there – in diplomatic-speak – as *demandeurs* too. What were we demanding?

I took the opportunity to make the case that the root of the problem was the government's perceived misrepresentation of the priority it attached to the 'creative industries' over the arts. I had prepared a short statement of less than two minutes on the subject as agreed with Dennis Stevenson who cued me in at the appropriate time:

'There is a real perception deficit about the government's approach to the arts. Over the last decade, the extent to which the arts play an important part in economic regeneration, job creation and tourism has become well understood, evaluated and costed. Phrases such as "cultural industries", "creative industries", evolved as a way of dragging arts subsidy funding in on the coat-tails of those commercial offshoots of the arts.

'In practice, the subsidised arts and the creative industries are part of a continuum of activities, skills and attitudes. They inter-relate, interact and feed into and off one another in a constructive, informal way. What has happened under this government is that – by design or inadvertence – a knife has been put between the subsidised arts and the creative industries. The latter have been held up as publicly and economically valuable, and an integral part of the re-branding Britain exercise; the former held up as less valuable, less relevant to New Labour's reformist project, more costly, and backward- rather than forward-looking.

'I know that this perception – or misperception – is widely felt by the arts world and by the public at large. I suggest that it does the government no good and the arts much harm that it is allowed to persist. I believe that it can be healed but it needs the government's own words and actions to show that it values the arts not because they need subsidy but because in the widest sense that subsidy is an investment in the nation's spirit.'

The debate broadened, after a marvellously idealistic state-ment from Richard Eyre, whose public status has become that of resident defender of values and seer of the non-material (but not immaterial). The arts world was looking for a recognition that the arts are not a commodity and cannot be treated as if they were part of the market in commercial arts. We wanted acknowledgement, too, that the arts have been under-funded for years and that the grant of subsidy does not by itself mean that the money is spent wastefully.

We asked at least for the arts to be treated on a par with sport – sports activity in schools is regarded as a key to the national health; but why is arts activity not seen in exactly the same light? 'Art is at the heart of the nation's health,' said one participant. Arts are essential to ease the nation's 'poverty of spirit'. Another stated roundly that the arts had been marginalised and under-funded for years by successive governments and it was time for this to stop.

In return, the arts side recognised that we needed to play our part in creating a new compact with the nation as well as with the government. 'There is a democratic deficit in the management of the arts,' said one of those present. Someone else urged arts institutions to be more confident in the skills they had within themselves and to offer those skills to the outside community.

But we did not just examine the philosophical basis of the position of arts in society. We discussed money, not in terms of volumes of pounds and pence alone but in terms of strategy. Lottery money must continue to be additional to the Treasury's contribution from national taxation revenues. The Lottery grant cannot be endlessly cannibalised to make up for the sustained shortcomings of the basic grant in aid.

I summed up what my artistic colleagues had told me they regarded as four essential elements in a finanancial 'Blair Settlement' for the arts. First, restore the value of the arts grant to what it was before the cash standstill four years ago. Second, give the arts a fixed annual grant which included an annual uplift for inflation. Third, give the arts a three-year settlement, allowing freedom to plan for more than one year at a time. Finally, tell us that from now on we are on our own. Anyone who could not manage on that basis would deserve whatever came to them.

I am breaking no confidence in saying that I and others thought that the Prime Minister used a very significant phrase in his summing up – it has already been reported in the press. 'We must write the arts into our core script,' he offered.

I gave two examples of other political leaders who had 'written the arts into their core scripts' and embodied them into their own core public acts. The former President of the Federal German Republic, Richard von Weizsäcker, would fly from Bonn to West Berlin to attend the opening of the Deutsche Oper's latest production of Wagner's *Ring* cycle. When Pierre Boulez was lured back to France to set up his musical research centre, IRCAM, in the Baubourg (the Pompidou Centre), he had been personally wooed by President Pompidou at a private dinner.

Will Tony Blair be as naturally inclined to interleave the arts into his core script in his own appropriate way?

Was the sense of mutual understanding at the seminar between the government and the arts real or had we been enmeshed in the web of the spinmasters? Remember what happened before the budget, said one wary participant. There was a leak that the Chancellor of the Exchequer, Gordon Brown, was going to find £40 million to 'save the museums'. On budget day, what they actually got was £6 million, but so tied up with conditions that, as one senior Whitehall hand observed with relish, 'it was a three card trick; now they saw it, now they didn't'.

So as we came out of Downing Street, we knew that the government had listened to the arts; but would they hear? Two weeks later we knew that they had done both. Gordon Brown's comprehensive survey of government public spending yielded £290 million extra for the arts over three years. When Chris Smith, the Culture Secretary, announced the details, the news that the newly-structured Arts Council would have £30 million, £40 million and £55 million extra in each of the next three years revealed a significant evolution in the government's attitude towards funding the arts.

What caused the change of mind and what part did the Downing Street Seminar play in it? Undoubtedly a primary reason for the transformation was that the arts world made a fuss. Whether it was another outburst from Sir Peter Hall or Sir John Drummond in his now-celebrated Royal Philharmonic Society lecture in January 1998, singly and collectively these very public questionings of the Blair Government's approach to the arts first ruffled Downing Street, then disturbed it, and finally drew ministers into action. There was a good measure of brutal political calculation involved. 'Look,' said a highly-placed Blair adviser to a musical friend, 'neither Brown nor his Treasury team are remotely interested in the arts and Tony isn't wildly interested himself. But they don't like the fuss, they see it will not go away and if a few million will buy it off, then it's worth paying.'

Against this background, the Arts Seminar had a specific function to fulfil. We had to convince Tony Blair that the arts world was a serious group of people; that we were professional about looking after money as well as delivering our particular art form. 'Prime Minister,' said Dennis Stevenson at one point in the meeting, 'everybody around this table runs an arts institution efficiently and effectively. That is one of the reasons that they are here.'

I suspect that the presence of the Paymaster General, Geoffrey Robinson, showed that sums of money for the arts had already been pencilled into the Comprehensive Spending Review. Whether figures at the higher end or the lower end of the range finally emerged in Gordon Brown's statement would be affected by how the arts world showed itself at the seminar.

I believe that the seminar worked, too, because of some shrewd handling by Chris Smith. While the Treasury and Downing Street can see – and see off – a 'give us more money' campaign at several leagues' distance, no one could trace Smith's fingerprints back to the general outcry from the arts. Yet there is no doubt that the Culture Ministry quietly fanned the voices of protest once it knew that Downing Street's anxieties had been aroused. These discreetly encouraged public protests both strengthened the case for the arts themselves and probably saved the ministerial skin of Chris Smith.

The Culture Secretary deserves credit at another level. For months, as the arts protests grew, Smith remonstrated that we should be patient and wait for the outcome of the Spending Review. No one paid much attention or believed in his capacity to deliver, but the final outcome proved him more right than many had believed possible.

One hopes that Tony Blair took away some serious messages from the seminar. First, that arts and museums make their own justification for subsidy. Subsidy is not a second best to the workings of the market but a vital factor in its own right, creating stability in institutions that foster innovation and high artistic standards. Second, that funding without an uplift for inflation for four years – cuts in everything but name – had predictably caused an acute financial crisis and Lottery money would not solve it. Third, that the arts world had to develop what Richard Eyre had identified as a 'new contract for the arts' between government, the people and the arts institutions.

But this Prime Minister always insists on something for something. In return for a large boost for arts funding, the Government is demanding action. Not just in the well-worn areas of excellence, access, education and economic development, but over actual reform. The arts must deliver better decisions, provide evidence of a clear strategy, ensure an end to bail-outs for the incompetent or terminally indecisive. Above all, the arts world must hope to be speedily delivered from the malignant shadow of the continuing mismanagement by the Royal Opera which Downing Street is not alone in seeing as having harmed every other arts institution.

The dialogue did not end at the doors of Downing Street. We were all invited, on that occasion and later by letter, to write to the Prime Minister with further observations on the state of the arts. After a good deal of thought over the summer, I decided to concentrate on an area that had not arisen at the seminar, that was not generally linked to the arts but which was central to the success of the arts: that is to say the roles of the broadcasters. They have a major responsibility to the arts. They were getting away scot free from scrutiny in this area. So, in September 1998, I wrote to Tony Blair turning his attention to this overlooked area of arts policy.

I am concentrating on a subject that did surface at the seminar – the relationship between education and the arts, to which you refer in your letter – but I want to add a further, so far missing, ingredient to the discussion which could even be its missing link. Fortunately, this falls squarely into the remit of Chris Smith's department – it is the role of broadcasting and the responsibility of the broadcasters in relation to the arts.

The damaging effect that cuts in music education have had in producing a generation deprived of basic access to music in the curriculum is well known. Simon Rattle and others have spoken to you eloquently about this. But the role of the broadcasters in enabling access and education about the arts to occur has been largely overlooked. It is curious that the broadcasters have stood aloof, in practice and in theory, in the very intense debate that the arts have been having with government in the last year or so. I think this is a grave, though perhaps not an accidental, omission on their part.

'The fact is that in the area of television, there has been a massive retreat from arts coverage journalistically, and from arts programming over the last decade. While the BBC has always played the greatest role in the area of arts promotion, one would expect it to do so as an essential part of its public service remit. Indeed, in the past, it has shouldered this responsibility freely and enthusiastically. It is the BBC's retreat from the arts which is the most glaring, both in radio and television.

'Put simply, if the broadcast media only broadcast news about the arts when there is a scandal, if they do not treat the arts as an essential part of society and social activity; if they have no language for addressing arts and their audiences and regard them as a vulnerable and undesirable part of the programme mix, then the audiences of the future are denied access to the arts because they will have received no education or information about them.

'A review of the way in which all TV and radio arts coverage has declined drastically in recent years is simple to carry out and would be instructive and alarming. Without improved coverage from the broadcasters, the commitment to reintroduce music education into schools is seriously weakened. The arts community can only do so much in the area of access to and education about the arts. Without a positive and active role from the broadcasters, much of your strategy to put the arts at the core of your political concerns and public interests is weakened.

'I urge you and Chris Smith to engage the broadcasting

authorities – privately or publicly – in discussion about their responsibility to the encouragement of the arts. In the case of the BBC, this discussion should centre on their proclaimed role and special responsibility as a public service broadcaster. But I do not think that the commercial broadcasters should be allowed to wriggle off the hook of arts provision on the grounds that they must maximise audiences, advertising and income.

'I believe that the progressive retreat from a convinced commitment to arts broadcasting – of the arts and about the arts – is an important factor in the steady decline in audiences. The arts world cannot address access and education by itself – the broadcasters have a role and responsibility and it seems to me and others essential that they acknowledge it and take it up. From your government's point of view, a three-way partnership between government, the arts, the private sector would be vastly strengthened by the involvement of the broadcasters. We would move from an unstable triangle to a soundly based square. Honestly, I do not believe you – or we – can do it without the broadcasters.'

There is, in short, still a long way to go before all the forces that can create a healthy, varied, dynamic arts world have been mobilised. There is a wholeness to the ecology of the arts world; the broadcasters are an integral part of it, but are too often treated as if they are mere observers. Trying to make artists and the arts institutions healthy by themselves only addresses, at best, two-thirds of the problem. Unless the broadcasters are part of the diagnosis and part of the solution, then the arts will always be struggling against much of the prevailing zeitgeist. Only government can make sure that the broadcasters play their parts in enhancing education about the arts, easing access and allowing familiarisation with what the arts have to offer. Without them, it will be an uphill struggle.

So Downing Street did start the dialogue between politicians

and the arts. Only an optimist would claim that it was more than
the end of the beginning.

8 When Being Creative is Not Enough*

It was rash of Chris Smith to put down his thoughts on the arts just when early hopes were fading that Labour might be the salvation of an arts community well and truly on the ropes. After all, the Tories had been notorious philistines. True, Margaret Thatcher had a Henry Moore maquette at Number 10; John and Norma Major were regular opera-goers (or rather Covent-Garden-goers, a somewhat different proposition). But by and large, the Tories – if they went to anything cultural – felt more at home with the smart and exclusive.

Not that Labour MPs were widely visible at plays or concerts, come to that, nor were MPs of any stripe or persuasion. There is a case for early closing in the Commons on one night a week with an obligation on MPs to attend something cultural, preferably in their own constituency. They would certainly understand the arts better and might be better politicians into the bargain. While such a dramatic shift of attitude and habit was too much to expect of New Labour, many would-be Labour courtiers in the arts during the Opposition wilderness years had convinced themselves that a new government would be both different from the Tories and better for the arts. They had to be, didn't they?

Well, the arts world – Labour, LibDem or Tory – soon discovered that just because Labour under Harold Wilson had created the first ever Arts Ministry where Jennie Lee gained an iconic reputation for what an arts minister should be, that was no guarantee that a new Labour government – or rather a 'NEW Labour' government (not quite the same thing) – would pick up

* Chris Smith's book *Creative Britain* was published in May 1998.

the reins where Jennie Lee had set them down. At this critical moment of burgeoning disillusion in the arts world in the summer of 1998, Chris Smith's book appeared. It was greeted with howls of derision, bordering on hate, and not just from leaders in the arts. All the frustrations, and more, felt by the beleaguered art world spilled out into the reviews. What was the book's crime? That it was not a paean of belief in the arts; it was not a cultural manifesto or personal credo, nor a statement of philosophy. It was a compendium of speeches, a *tour d'horizon*, a workmanlike departmental summary, in effect, of his efforts to date as Secretary of State for Culture, Media and Sport.

Much water has flowed under the bridge since that lurid publication day in the summer of 1998, but neither the book nor its philosophy has been disowned by the author or his government. Since the operating principles and beliefs it describes are still valid and must be assumed to drive government policies to the arts, both deserve a more considered examination. My own view is that the book is by no means as bad as the reviewers suggested, but that good or bad, better or worse, it cannot simply be rejected. If it describes the approach of the government of the day and of the foreseeable future, the arts world had better take it into account in framing its own expectations and behaviour.

For a start, Chris Smith's heart is clearly in the right place. He says a lot of the right things – I mean things that reflect an interest in and respect for the arts as something necessarily distinct from other activities and to be valued because they are different. That is a good start.

He repudiates 'Cool Britannia' as a slogan for the government's approach to the arts. But he is extremely disingenuous in blaming media reporting and wilful misinterpretation by outsiders for the misunderstanding surrounding that glib phrase and the derision heaped on it. Government spokesmen enthusiastically adopted the term and assiduously deployed it so long as it suited them. As soon as even the pop stars, who were at the heart of the 'Cool Britannia' phenomenon, objected to the phrase and their exploitation by it, the government backed off very fast.

Smith's public rejection of it is part of that process. Still, rejected it is.

He gives several reasons for defending state subsidy of the arts (yet oddly omits enabling the arts to continue to exist as one of them). He sets out specific ways in which culture and creativity make a vital contribution to a healthy society. He recognises the value of the English language to Britain – an asset that others will seize as their own instrument of international communication while we often undervalue it as our own national means of expression and the definer of our identity. He is not afraid of the idea or practice of preserving heritage – a ball and chain of a concept that right-wingers strapped onto the arts, and that left-wing populists found it convenient to kick pejoratively. He accepts the concept of 'heritage' as a simple acknowledgement that the achievements of the past, particularly its physical monuments, are worthy of respect and maintenance.

Smith has a nifty line in using uplifting quotations (hats off to the Department's reference library, no doubt), carefully rationed out on a speech-by-speech basis. I hope he has restored some of them to the general currency of public debate. Each one makes a contribution to the case for the necessity, the legitimacy, of the arts.

Thus, Hazlitt: 'The arts do not furnish us with food or raiment, it is true; but they please the eye, they haunt the imagination, they solace the heart. If after that you ask the question, *Cui bono?* there is no answer to be returned.' It may be difficult and unfashionable to make an absolute claim like that a hundred years after Hazlitt, but it remains one worth attempting.

George Bernard Shaw is invoked: 'The statesman should rank fine art with, if not above, religion, science, art education and fighting power as a political agency.' But fifty years after GBS's hortation, it remains just that: an ideal rather than a reality. Commitment to the 'fine arts' ranks lower in governmental concerns than it did when GBS wrote. And Smith includes some neat, contemporary quotes to show that the search for the conclusive argument in favour of the arts is a continuing mission. For example, it was the Gulbenkian Foundation that said: 'The

arts are the principal trainers of imagination.' Smith himself
carried over a personal observation when he changed portfolios
from Health to the Arts: 'Health is a *sine qua non*; but culture is a
raison d'être.' Yet, while these statements are raised like well-
meaning flags of principle to show where the author stands, his
ultimate failure to attach policies to such principles makes them
appear like mere flags of convenience rather than active calls to
the colours.

In another area of his departmental responsibility, Chris Smith
makes practical points about the new era of multi-channel TV
and the BBC's role in it. As a strong supporter of public service
broadcasting, he sees the BBC role as the benchmark of quality
programme making – a role which is more not less essential in an
'era of viewing choice'. He insists that viewers want to watch
good programmes rather than themed channels; channels are,
after all, a technological and marketing construct. Programmes
provide viewing in audience-friendly sizes and formats. More
recently, in an article in the *Radio Times* in September 1998,
Smith has written with even greater emphasis about the
importance of the BBC remaining a programme-driven organisation: 'If the BBC continues to produce high-quality programmes,
it will be difficult for other channels, who require an additional
payment, to offer something inferior and get away with it.' And
he added a significant warning: 'I've told [BBC] senior management that the judgement by government and public will be based
primarily on quality, not ratings.' Taking his book and these
subsequent statements together, the Blair Government's uncritical endorsement of the market-driven, multi-channel-directed
policies of Bland and Birt at the BBC looks very odd. On this
evidence, BBC bosses are significantly out of kilter with what
Smith himself believes about the primacy of programme excellence as the Corporation's main function. Equally, the BBC's
obsession with research-driven, ratings-directed programme making sits uneasily with such a clear direction from their political
master.

The BBC is not the only subject where the more you read
Creative Britain, the more the questions and doubts crowd in. For

instance: in the government's continuing insistence on the need for accessibility the arts are implicitly reproached for making themselves remote, exclusive and inaccessible. Yet this is to beat a horse that does not exist. One or two corporate subscribers to Covent Garden may have stated freely in the notorious television documentary *The House* that they wanted their clients to feel they were coming somewhere exclusive, but I know of no one in the arts, or in a serious audience, who wants to keep anybody else away from a performance. Rather the opposite: we clamour to get people in and are active in devising programmes and pricing strategies to help that to happen.

At the same time, however, certain things cannot be made more intellectually accessible than they are. Four-and-a-half hours of Wagner or Messiaen's *St Francis of Assisi* are just that; long, and difficult as well. Such masterpieces, and many others, are supremely worth the effort. If to be accessible involves making an artistic event easier than was its creator's intention, then the call for 'accessibility' is a call for the removal of most of the things that make a work into a work of art. I know Chris Smith neither believes that nor wants that to happen. Yet the facile chanting of the 'access' mantra slides away from facing up to its complex implications.

The real problem is less one of approachability than of an indifference to or actual rejection of the arts by wide sections of society. This reflects a generation of educational practice where the historic arts – to coin a phrase – have been undervalued because they have been labelled by some educational theorists and teachers as 'inaccessible', 'irrelevant' and a variety of other pejorative words. If the government truly cares about the arts, it must address the problem of 'rejection' quite as energetically as the one they now choose to emphasise: that of 'access'. The latter is the symptom; the former is the cause of the problem. Of course, the cure might be a different mantra – education, education, education – but that would depend on what is put into the educational curriculum.

But the fundamental weakness of the Smith philosophy is the all-inclusiveness of his definitions. It is all very well – or not very well – to set aside as too remote from everyday experience Matthew Arnold's definition of culture as embracing 'the best that has been known and said in the world'. But to slip into preferring Bobby Kennedy's shallow definition of culture as 'that which make life worthwhile' – as Chris Smith does – is to believe that playing tag football around the pool at Camelot, or sleeping with Marilyn, is culture. Enjoyable of course; but culture? In any case, the Kennedy clan are unreliable witnesses to enlist in the support of the arts. After a performance on the White House lawn by the pipes and drums of the Black Watch, Jackie Kennedy confided in a staffer: 'The President really enjoyed himself. He did suffer so when Casals played here.'

So too the inherent dangers of these over-stretched definitions are exposed in the use of the key Smith word 'creative'. I can see why he wants to rescue the word from the constriction of being used to describe, say, only Shakespeare, Tolstoy, Michelangelo and Picasso and never anyone lower in the pantheon or anything other than the most original and intense acts of artistic creation. This is the Himalayan application of the word that leaves 99.9% of humanity stigmatised with the label of 'uncreative'.

But in this rescue attempt, Smith credits almost every activity with any element of individual thought with being 'creative'. Advertising? Of course. Videos and television, naturally. Antiques? Up to a point. Fashion? You bet. Computer games? Certainly. Would he include 'creative accounting' too? Of course there is a 'creative' element in all of these activities, but when all are wrapped up in the same word, it rapidly loses any real value. Is the creativeness applied in all these widely diverse activities really the same?

And sooner rather than later, Smith faces the tricky question. If these activities – useful, enjoyable, entertaining as they are – are creative, what are the arts? Are they more creative than the above, just as creative, or less creative? He does not say. Are they – harder still – different in their creativity from the 'creative industries'? He does not attempt an answer. For the great evasion in the Smith book is that he never addresses the question of the real distinctiveness of art. He hoped to dodge the question by making the word 'creative' all-embracing. But the wider the doors are opened, the more glaring is the scale of his evasion.

For the arts get left behind in the crush to get through the doors of inclusiveness, especially as earning money appears to be part of the price of the entry ticket. 'Creative industries' – as defined by Chris Smith – are sometimes original, often ingenious and frequently inventive. They are also lucrative, or if not then they go out of business. Some arts – or certainly some artists – get rich. But does failure to make money from your work disqualify you from being considered an artist? And if an artist does not make ends meet, does this necessarily invalidate his work? If an arts institution does not earn its keep, does it fail to qualify for the accolade of being part of the 'creative industries'? In these thickets Smith does not go hunting. He has no way through them. But the thickets are of his own planting.

The trouble is that he will not come clean. What is art? And does he value it even if it is not a creative industry? Recently, Chris Smith declined to differentiate between 'high and low art' because he said that would involve making a value judgement! Does he make no value judgements as a politician or as a private individual? What is the point of being Secretary of State for Culture if you will not risk making some value judgements? To highlight the importance of the creative industries, to celebrate British achievements in them, and to mark the extent to which they are a truly post-industrial part of the modern economy are all useful activities. But they are matters that sound more like the province of the Department of Trade and Industry.

And the more Chris Smith talks of these industries, the further we are from the arts. Do they matter because they are good for the soul? Are they useful as a kind of social purgative, like rhubarb? Do they have an intrinsic value that society needs to encourage if it is to stay more than a materialist creation? Do they matter at all? If so, how much are they worth, and do they repay the cost? Specifically, how much are they worth to New Labour? Answers are needed to such questions if Britain is to have an arts policy and a flourishing arts world which will last far,

far longer than 'Cool Britannia', 'Creative Britain' or 'Rebrand-
ing Britain' – which are merely modish diversions. If Chris Smith
could answer the fundamental questions about art, he might find
that the creative industries flourished even more as a result.

9 Thoughts on the Thoughts of Chairman Gerry*

Not long ago, a leading British arts institution was looking for a finance director. There was a good response to the advertisements. Half the applicants came from the City and business worlds, from people who had done their stint there and fancied that the arts would make a more pleasant working environment for the rest of their lives. A massive drop in salary could easily be reconciled with a significant increase in quality of life-satisfaction. This was encouraging. At the formal interview, the attitude of the majority of these business applicants was less so. All explained in turn that they saw their mission as being to help the arty folks do their sums. It was, after all, well known in business circles that arts people could not add up; fortunately, help was at hand in the shape of people who could. Unsurprisingly, no one who took this attitude was appointed.

That experience – not an isolated one – points to the demons that block the road to understanding between arts bureaucrats and arts practitioners. The new Chairman of the Arts Council of England, Gerry Robinson, Chairman of the Granada Group, lamented in his inaugural Arts Council Lecture in October 1998: 'Some have seen the appointment of a businessman to the Chairmanship of the Arts Council as a threat to the very life-blood of the arts.' True enough, and his lecture did not do as much as it might to assuage those anxieties. But, as he unconsciously revealed in that lecture, his own view of the arts world is peopled with demons of misperception: 'We will no longer tolerate an assumption too widely held across the arts in

* The Arts Council Lecture was delivered in October 1998.

the past,' he thundered in a rather excessively business corporate tone, 'that artistic excellence is somehow a substitute for proper management or that sound financing is somehow too vulgar to be a concern.' It sounds as if a heavy schedule of meetings with arts leaders is needed to show him what a parody of reality that statement represents.

For the tone struck in the lecture is not a happy one: more a lecture at the arts than to them, still less a lecture about the arts. Perhaps a period of ideological disarmament is needed. The arts world will set aside its suspicion that Gerry Robinson regards subsidised clients as no different from loss-making catering subsidiaries – to be given five years to balance their books or shut up shop. In return, he will stop treating his arts clients as innumerate and profligate ninnies with permanent begging bowls as an extension of their right arms.

Yet all is not lost. There is a good deal that the new Chairman of the Arts Council gets right in his lecture. He recognises that the Lottery's 'Arts for Everyone' scheme – otherwise shortened to A4E – was a huge success in identifying an insatiable demand for grassroots participatory activity. Understandably, he places less emphasis on the way that the subsequent call for funding far exceeded the supply of cash available.

Robinson makes well the case for devolution of arts spending from the centralised dispensations of the Arts Council in Whitehall to the Regional Arts Boards. It is the spirit of the times, to be sure. He seems properly realistic about the caution with which the transfers of cash and responsibilities must be handled and the time it will take. Having made a reality of his promise of a 'bonanza for the regions' (to use his words) – with an increase in resources of no less than forty-four per cent in the Arts Council funding round in December 1998 – then the need to make sure that the newly enriched Regional Arts Boards do not spend those resources like drunken sailors moves towards the top of the ACE's own priorities. Judging by Gerry Robinson's words, it reads as if it will. His other comment, about the need to use the Arts Council as a body concerned with strategic decisions – presumably to look at arts as a whole rather than being tied up with particular companies and hard cases – will be tested against performance.

On easier ground, Robinson makes the now familiar and well accepted case for the arts as significant contributors to the physical and spiritual well-being of society. Do you want a distressed urban environment regenerated? Call in the arts. Do you want jobs created? Call in the arts. Do you want healthier patients in hospitals, more imaginative children in schools, a more lively response to treatment from the handicapped or the elderly? Call in the arts. Too often these calls sound no different from the tired old aguments for the arts made by those ashamed to make claims for them in themselves.

A large part of the lecture is devoted to the facts and figures quantifying the economic benefits associated with the arts. Employment in the 'cultural industries' has grown by 34% in the decade from 1981 to 1991 against a mere 4.6% in general employment. (You would of course expect something like this in an economy shifting from traditional manual to thought-based industries.) Artists, sculptors, authors and designers now turn over £2.5 billion compared with £1.1 billion five years ago. Arts related tourism earns £2 billion a year for Britain, a fifth of the entire national earnings from tourism.

Admirable as these figures are, however, they remain peripheral to the big issue of why the arts should be funded at all, and funding the arts is the *raison d'être* of the Arts Council. Mozart is Mozart because of his music and not because he created a tourist industry in Salzburg or gave his name to decadent chocolate and marzipan Salzburger kugel. Picasso is important because he taught a century new ways of looking at objects and not because his paintings in the Bilbao Guggenheim Museum are regenerating an otherwise derelict northern Spanish port. Van Gogh is valued because of the pain or intensity of his images and colours, and not because he made sunflowers and wooden chairs popular. Absolute quality is paramount in attempting a valuation of the arts; all other factors are interesting, useful but secondary.

Still, if these are the yardsticks by which Gerry Robinson judges the arts, they should be welcomed and encouraged. What is not clear is how the Chairman will use the evidence that, like Guinness, 'The Arts are Good for You,' to make the case for increased government funding. His own declared priorities include a readiness to provide a 'more confident advocacy on behalf of the arts by the Arts Council'. We are left to wait and see how and when he does this. To judge by too much of the tone of the lecture, Robinson feels that the arts still need stern admonition – about management responsibility? – before he is ready to move into 'confident advocacy' on their behalf. It remains unclear at the end what the arts must do to be worthy of his 'confident advocacy'. How can we make him more confident?

When he has gained his confidence, what will he advocate? Still standing on the familiar ground, Robinson invokes the Blessed Trinity of 'Excellence, Education and Access'. The last has been so exhaustively and tiresomely worked over that it needs no further discussion here, except to wince that Robinson, in his 'the arts are bad-boys' mood, still voices the trite accusation that arts bodies spend more of their time keeping audiences out rather than getting them in. Education in the arts is now plugged to the point of banality. Yet the fact that he chose to use the Los Angeles Philharmonic as the paradigm of good educational outreach work, ignoring the role played by British practitioners in creating these very programmes at the LA Phil in their early days, was a revealing insight into his reluctance to give much credit to the British arts world. One can only hope that the angry response his lauding of the LA Phil drew from British arts educationists will have helped him to acknowledge that there are good examples to draw from in his own backyard. It is as if it is necessary to give the arts a bad name now so that he can get maximum credit for any subsequent improvement.

That leaves the first part of the Trinity of aspiration: excellence. The arts must be 'excellent'. To be sure. But what, apart from calling for excellence to be achieved, will he do as Chairman of the Arts Council of England to help the arts institutions to achieve it? His lecture leaves that fuzzy. Any theatre or dance company, any opera house, any orchestra, any arts centre can offer a list of things that are essential for artistic excellence to be created. But as he makes very clear, the Chairman is not interested in an 'assembly of wish lists from every part of the arts constituency'. For Gerry Robinson, 'We've seen that before and what a waste of effort it was.' But what about dreams, what about ideals, where is the room for visions, what place is left for ideas? Is there no place for them in this brave-ish new world? Excellence cannot be created without them. Must the arts bodies that create excellence set their visions aside just because the Chairman is impatient of what he calls 'wish lists', preferring 'a limited number of deliverable priorities' instead? Even on his own terms, how do you decide which 'deliverable priorities' you want to concentrate on unless you have dreamed a far longer list first and decided which you want to deliver first? I suspect Robinson is in a quandary because dreams, visions and ideas are unsound, unquantifiable arty language, whereas 'deliverable priorities' are robust, gritty and managerial. But no one has ever delivered artistic excellence through that sort of talk alone.

There is a further linguistic oddity in Gerry Robinson's lecture. In a word that reeks of Old Labour, he speaks of a 'check list of entitlements to the arts each citizen should be able to enjoy'. The very idea of blanket 'entitlements' without a corresponding contribution on the part of the citizen sits oddly with the rest of New Labour rhetoric, in which they are the cause of so much of the problem: too many people expecting too much 'as of right' and acknowledging their responsibility for creating benefits too little. What can these 'entitlements to arts' mean – no one further than twenty miles from a cinema, fifty miles from a theatre, a hundred miles from an orchestra, a hundred and fifty miles from an opera company? Perhaps there could be a subsidised 'arts voucher' scheme, cashable at a specified list of publicly funded arts institutions.

Not that it is clear that this approach to deciding arts priorities will yield anything much but vague pieties of the 'let's all love one another' variety. Soon after Robinson's lecture – in November 1998 – the world marked the fiftieth anniversary of the Universal Declaration of Human Rights. Close examination of some of the more obscure clauses – such as those guaranteeing everyone a job – show how tragically pointless such global assertions of priorities can be. Urgent they have been, for more than half a century; but they have proved to be undeliverable.

Another no-nonsense manager, Greg Dyke, was called in by the government to revise the Patients' Charter for the National Health Service. In December 1998, after a year's work, the end result appeared to be the assertion that everyone should have access to high quality health care; local health organisations should be efficient; professionals and patients should work together; and communications should be open. A lot of patients could have been treated in the time that such a collection of truisms was cobbled together. Let us hope that the Arts Council's list of arts 'deliverable priorities' will turn out to be more practicable than those for the wretched patients, and that they are informed by a stronger sense of what it will cost to deliver them.

As my contribution to the national debate that the Chairman says he wants, I suggest that a list of arts entitlements should surely include the following: the right to be taught about the arts at their widest in school and at college; the right to free access to museums and galleries; the right to affordable tickets for theatre, concerts, dance and opera; some right to access to such activities within manageable distances; some right to more than the occasional annual visit to one of the foregoing. Should this be dismissed as just my 'wish list'? Or should it be welcomed as Gerry Robinson's 'check list of entitlements'? Call it what you want, the question of what either might cost is the interesting one. Dreaming of entitlements is the easy part. What citizens should have is a far cry from what the state can afford to give them.

There are crucial antitheses that await reconciliation. They surface on the last page of his lecture, when Robinson makes a heartfelt plea for an end to 'bogus debates'. Like Chris Smith, he asserts that there is no contradiction between popular art and high art, between art as an economic motor for society and art as self-expression for the creative individual. If only this were true. The fact is that such questions are at the core of all the current arguments. Wishing them absent does not make them vanish even if they could. As part of his own contribution to the national arts debate, Gerry Robinson might reflect far harder on how these antitheses could be reconciled. He might also look back at his lecture and ask himself why so much of it is couched in terms that reflect the polarisation, of which he says he disapproves, rather than those that assist the synthesisation of differences, which is what he says he wants.

For, and also worryingly, at the front of Gerry Robinson's mind there is a schizophrenic view of the arts. This is reflected in a glaring contradiction in the text. Early on, he berates the arts for having the patronising view 'in the back of their minds . . . the vague hope that one day enlightenment might descend semi-miraculously upon the rest, that the masses might one day get wise to their brilliance'. Yet later in the lecture he states approvingly, as if it were his own contribution to human understanding, that 'the gateway to Birtwhistle [sic] and Cage can be Strauss and Mozart. A love of Betjeman can lead to appreciation of T. S. Eliot and Simon Armitage.' Many in the arts would agree with him, even while being a good deal more reserved about just how the transmission belt of appreciation works. He could have chosen to give the arts credit for having reached this conclusion long before he did, rather than elevating it to just another item in the charge sheet against them.

At the end, Robinson calls for a clearing away of the undergrowth so that a landscape is created where the arts can flourish. Let us hope that the scrub removed includes a number of the prejudices and preconceptions contained in this lecture. Then the debate about the arts that Gerry Robinson says he wants can really start.

Part Three: Actions

10 Art for Art's Sake – Art! for Heaven's Sake

This is my credo. I believe in management. I believe in the bottom line. I believe in the vision and mission statement. I believe in objectives. I believe in the box office. I believe in strategy. And I believe in marketing. At the Barbican we were the first arts organisation to use so-called 'mapping' and 'mosaic' techniques for the identification and targeting of audience groups. But we believe in good, appropriate and relevant research, not bad, inappropriate and externally imposed research. That is the distinction we must insist on. For first of all is my credo. I believe in art for art's sake; or better still, I believe in Art! for Heaven's Sake.

That's it, then? All problems solved? Well, not quite. Because you can't believe in all these things, at least not at the same time or in exactly the same way. Art, like socialism, is about the language of priorities. If we set aside the fact that all too often the first priority for the art world in Britain is plain survival, we can at least agree to put art first. And then we can ask 'what must we do for art to be saved?'

To pursue the religious theme for a moment more; when Christ was asked by the young man what he had to do to be saved, he replied: 'Sell everything you have and give it to the poor.' Today, that is the appeal that the arts world makes to the rich: 'Sell some of what you have and give it to us.' Many private benefactors do just that, both personally and institutionally. They are not obliged to do so. It is marvellous that they do. The arts world should not assume that they will. Britain is a long way from having the notion of citizenship, or the structure of personal taxation, that would create a culture of personal giving on anything like an American scale. But if arts funding is to continue to flourish it will need a variety of sources to rely on and a significant growth in personal giving will need to take place. Whether the Treasury's rules on the taxation of charitable giving will make that easier remains open to doubt.

How positive it would be if some of the higher Lottery winners used their money to help the arts in the places where they live. Since the Lottery started in November 1994, more than seven hundred people have won individual prizes of more than £1 million each, some considerably more than a million. It would be impertinent for anyone to suggest to the lucky seven hundred – and counting – how to spend their money, a windfall that transforms their lives. But what additional pleasure they might have had from sharing a tiny part of their good fortune with others by sponsoring a concert, a play or some other arts activity taking place within their community. Not only would they have supported an important local institution and given enjoyment to hundreds or thousands of their friends and neighbours, but they would have discovered the delights of supporting the arts, in whatever form they chose, for themselves. Perhaps Camelot and the Regional Arts Boards could set up a small counselling group to show interested Lottery winners that they could get real satisfaction, and a warm glow of generosity, by moving in this direction. As it is, they are offered advice on how to invest their money. Suggestions on how to use a small part of it in a socially enriching way would enlighten a small part of the arts landscape.

But while the arts must look for support wherever they can, they are not beggars. Self-help, self-sacrifice have always been an intrinsic part of their lives. So when they ask themselves 'what must we do to be saved?' the answer is at once more simple and more complex. 'Help yourself,' is what it boils down to, and I don't mean in the sense of helping ourselves to money that others – whether in the state or the private sector – have supplied. It does mean helping ourselves by making the best of the skills and disciplines that management and financial tools, mission-statements and marketing offer us. But it has to be in that order: art comes first, the skills second. We must not get the relationship the wrong way round, and there are signs that some people believe that the substance of business techniques is more important in the arts world than the real matter of the arts. That is what worries me.

So what is art? Or perhaps what are the arts that we are all in the business of devising, creating, promoting, marketing and selling? First, arts are not entertainment in the sense that a ten screen cinema complex and bowling alleys are entertainment. The cinema complex may well be screening a film that is judged to be artistic, but run-of-the-mill movie-going is far closer to mere diversion rather than anything more profound. (This is not to downgrade film as art but merely to observe that most films watched by us most of the time are not even straying into artistic territory.) Besides, the modern film industry is classically the child of the marketeers. Where is the mass audience perceived to be? Youth. What kind of things do they want to see? Action. What action leaps over language barriers? Violence and disasters. What makes money? Youth-oriented, disaster movies with minimal language content, where a fist or a Kalashnikov are the principal forms of communication. What do you do when you or another studio has made a winner to this formula? Make another one just like it.

The fact that this road, however scrupulously mapped, often leads to financial, never mind artistic, disaster does not stop it being followed. The arts, by contrast, may sometimes be imitative, but they cannot be formulaic or market-chasing in this way – or not if they hope to survive. Their imperatives must be the idea, the original, the creative, the unexpected, the different. Double standards operate here. When an arts centre runs up a deficit of a few hundred thousand pounds, the air is thick with charges of bad management and artistic indulgence. Few attempts are made to relate the loss to the ambition of the arts programming. Yet when a major Hollywood studio loses tens of millions on a single film, this is seen as a necessary characteristic of the industry's search for success. Mismanagement is never raised as an issue.

It should always be borne in mind that the arts have a

different, perhaps inconvenient, view of the way we live and
behave. Professor Susan Greenfield, the authority on the human
brain, recently expressed concern about two aspects of modern
life: the CD-ROM, and our constant search for sensation. Young
people now, she argued, press a button on their CD-ROM and
get instant gratification. It is, metaphorically and literally, 'in
their face'. They are confronted by a visual image; in a sense it is
imposed on them. Previous generations had, she asserted, to use
their imaginations more. When she was asked why using the
imagination was better than immediate access to the inconceiv-
ably rich supply of information that the CD-ROM can provide,
Professor Greenfield said: 'Because it gives you an attention span
exceeding a few micro-seconds. It gives you the power to escape
from the present. If you don't have an imagination, then you
can't interpret what you see.' On her theory of how the mind
works, the arts are an essential part of that process of
interpretation, harnessing the imaginative world to make better
sense of life around us.

Susan Greenfield then argued that if life is principally directed
to the pursuit of pleasure – whether raving, bungee-jumping,
chewing – then you abandon the past, detach yourself from the
future and, in merely blowing your mind, ultimately abrogate
your personality. This is a strong warning from an academic
observer of the brain and how we use it. But her observations are
central to an understanding of what the arts world is trying to
make available to society. They define the importance to society
of an activity which swims against the tide, goes against the
current of so much of the rest of human social life.

If the arts are not allowed to stimulate and engage the
imagination, to connect the present with the past and the future,
to provoke reflection, then the purely entertaining and diversionary side of human activity will produce more and more of
what Greenfield calls 'flat personalities – those who seek instant
gratification, in booze, drugs or violence', because they do not
know anything better. On this view, when the arts provide an
alternative vision of life to the prevailing one of material

gratification, they offer society an essential therapy whose social, never mind artistic, value cannot be over-estimated.

None of this is to say or to believe that taking part in the arts involves wearing a permanent spiritual and intellectual hair shirt. The arts are, of course, intensely enjoyable. But that pleasure at its best comes as the result of some personal attention and engagement, some commitment of time, thought and emotion. There is violence in Wagner's *Ring* cycle: destruction, immolation, not to mention incest, treachery, murder and most of the rest of human life. It takes time to get to the final cataclysm – literally days. It can be a shattering experience, but only because the terminal act of destruction springs from an immensely complex set of human and moral actions which lead inexorably to the climactic minutes of overwhelming sensation. The experience of appreciation involves more than sensation; understanding is at issue and understanding takes time; it does not come and hit you on the head. And it is that steady, sometimes slow, sometimes tiresome search for a kind of revelation that the arts must be involved in.

In short, much of what the arts offer is unpopular with, and seen as antipathetic to, the predominant drift of society. To many, they are just plain unfashionable. That will always raise problems for marketeers. And the big one they have to face is that it is when the arts have been at their most shocking and unpopular that they have laid the seeds for their greatest subsequent successes. Stravinsky's *Rite of Spring* caused a riot when it was first performed in 1913. It is now a standard classic and crowd pleaser. Harold Pinter's *The Birthday Party* was judged incomprehensible by every critic – except Harold Hobson of the *Sunday Times* – when it was first performed in 1957. Forty years ago, Mahler and Bruckner were spoken of as if they were twin composers in style, and united in irrelevance and inaccessibility to the general musical public. Where would the concert hall be today without the regular dose of Mahler giganticism?

Three years ago, nobody advised Clive Gillinson, Managing Director of the London Symphony Orchestra, and Sir Colin Davis, its Principal Conductor, that they should perform the full cycle of Bruckner symphonies on the centenary of his death. They expected to lose money on the project but felt it was an artistic effort worth making. In the event, the cycle triumphed both artistically and financially. Who told John Christie that there was a market for high quality international opera at his country house at Glyndebourne? Who told Lilian Baylis that there was a market for drama and opera among the working population of inner London? In all these cases, and dozens more, artistic success came from a prior artistic perception, not from a marketing strategy or concern about where these institutions should 'position themselves'. Yet an instinctive awareness of the position they wanted to occupy – Christie with high quality performance in select surroundings, Baylis with good value performances for the less well-off – sprang from the basic artistic impulse. It was an integral part of the wish to create.

For many of those who conceived these great projects, marketing as we understand it today did not exist. They succeeded on their own terms. The lesson is surely clear. In the arts, the idea comes first, second and last as the motive for artistic activity. No one is proof against bad ideas or good ideas before their time. But without an idea to start with, the rest is a waste of time.

One of Glyndebourne's recent artistic and audience successes was Peter Sellars's modernist realisation of Handel's semi-oratorio, *Theodora*, first staged there in May 1996. I asked Anthony Whitworth-Jones, then Glyndebourne's General Director, how they had come to decide to do it. 'By market research among the existing audience?' I suggested hopefully. 'No,' he said. 'If we had asked the audience, "do you want to hear more Handel?" the answer would have been lukewarm. If we had said, "do you want to see *Theodora*?" they would have expressed fair ignorance of the work. If we had asked, "do you want to see *Theodora* produced by Peter Sellars, the man who did the controversial *Magic Flute*?" they would have given a resounding "No".' So how did he decide to do it? 'I thought Handel was a good idea and Peter suggested *Theodora*.' Elitist – possibly; authoritative – certainly; right – undoubtedly.

But of course the arts need marketing because what we are doing is comparatively difficult in a society where everything is made increasingly easy. Household chores are dealt with by labour-saving; a good thing too. Can the chore of paying attention to the arts be made easier by attention-saving? Writing in the *Guardian*, David McKie drew his readers' incredulous attention to a proposal that St Andrew's, the home of golf no less, should be the site of a brand new golf course, but one without bunkers. The fact that the bunker is part of the essence of the game, just as snakes are an essential part of Snakes and Ladders, is to be deliberately set aside. The new, modern sensibility appears to believe that bunkers make the game too difficult and families will not have a nice day out if they spend too much of their time thrashing away in a sand trap. But golf is difficult, life is hard and only a fool thinks that ladders are more a part of life's experience than snakes.

At the end, McKie observed that we 'live in a culture which wants to make everything easy, to say: "this is not going to hurt"; to turn sport into showbiz; to take the pain out of politics' – and he might have added 'out of art, too'. 'That is an unhealthy culture,' he went on, 'not least because it denies what many have learned, sometimes painfully, to be true; that there is often deeper satisfaction from things that come hard than from things that come easily.' That observation applies to the arts even more. There are no cheap thrills in art, but there are real thrills. They come slowly, gradually, over years, and as a result of effort. How do you market such an unappealing message, which happens to be the real message of the arts, the core – to use market-speak – of their 'Unique Selling Proposition'?

One of the difficulties in constructing a balanced relationship between arts and marketing lies in the instruments that marketeers use to get their information. Above all the focus on focus groups. The problem with them is that the members tell us what they want in the future on the basis of what they know now. How can it be otherwise? They are bound to express wishes or comments on the basis of their existing experiences. They are poorly equipped to indicate directions in which they might be willing to be led. Focus groups are poorly designed to be useful in showing where people might be ready to be taken by surprise. The danger is that they yield results that confirm the conservative, the anticipated, the existing and the customary. If they concentrate on wants rather than needs, the results will be skewed.

The arts must never forget that taste is led and formed by people who appreciate then deliberately go beyond the familiar. If the arts are to survive they must live in the area that marketing can never predict or marketing inquiry can never deliver. They cannot be defined, tailored, processed and packaged into shapes that are guaranteed to succeed. Neither risk nor financial loss can be eliminated. From time to time, a formula appears – say in music. For some years, the Albert Hall was filled every Sunday night with Tchaikovsky, climaxing with the 1812 overture. Marketing would have been in a seventh heaven. The perfect formula: popular, repeatable, predictable as to cost, risk and sales. Unfortunately, the formula, like all others, ran out of steam and out of audience. It was fun while it lasted but it could not last forever. Marketing could not give it new life; another idea was needed and will always be needed. Without an idea, marketing is just a bunch of statistics.

The revamp of BBC Radio 4 in 1998 was an interesting case in point. Never before had a controller been armed with so many statistics. Never before had so much research been done or been available. Never before had a controller offered fewer reasons for listeners to tune in, fewer thoughts for them to respond to, fewer new programmes other than slight variants on tired old generic, consumer-driven formulae such as gardening, leisure, food and travel. All the changes added up to was consumer research dressed up as ideas for programmes. The resulting network appeared to be driven by reliance on the audience's expressed requirements, not on an intelligent, sympathetic interpretation of their real needs. Of curiosity, invention, intellectual reach across, beyond or through the consumer categories to the audience's needs, there was no sign, and still less apparent inclination to venture into such territory.

This most recent instance of editorial responsibility prostrating itself before the focus groups, of common sense and acquired judgement bowing down before the supposed voice of the people, has proved a fickle guide to programming – which will come as no surprise except to those besotted with such research. Two cases vividly demonstrated how unreliable it is. In the first, 'research showed' – and executives spoke in hushed tones of the expense of conducting it – that the 9 a.m. news summary on Radio 4 caused a huge fall in listening at that time. The research-driven answer was to drop the summary and start the next programme on the dot of nine – audiences would 'obviously' carry over as a result. They did not. Only months later, the 9 a.m. news summary was reinstated in response to listeners' complaints.

In the second example, the same focus groups observed that they enjoyed a radio quiz show at around 1.30 p.m. So the entire 1–2 p.m. Radio 4 schedule was rejigged across the week to give listeners a radio quiz at 1.30 p.m. each day; it was 'what they wanted'. Again, within months, it was clear that listeners did not want this formula imposed on them, every single day of the week, and the project was re-shaped. There is a fundamental ideological puzzle here for the marketeers. How can the public in one guise, the focus group, voice a wish for certain types of programming; and then in another guise – that of angry-letter-writer – bitterly criticise the changes delivered as a result of those focus groups?

Clearly, these mistakes sprang from the theory that a programme can only exist if it fits with the answers to consumer questionnaires and into predestined categories. The new Radio 4 schedule was driven by one impulse: if the audience switched off, then there must be something wrong with the programme; if they did not switch on, there could be nothing right in it. Subjective perspicacity, professional acumen, the accumulated wisdom of experience, the ingredients of the editorial and creative process, are pushed to one side, made subservient, judged invalid by the iron laws of market research. If ever a relaunch of a major national cultural and artistic landmark such as BBC Radio 4 demanded a Vision and Mission Statement – those tools beloved of the management men – this was it. It was conspicuous by its absence.

When Gerard Mansell, the creator of today's Radio 4 in the late 1960s, reshaped what was a very pre-war sounding network, he knew all about the available audience research. But above all, he had an editorial sense of what he thought the network needed – and the audience would gobble up. The result of his editorial and journalistic hunch – working with that bred-in-the-bone newsman William Hardcastle – was the innovative programme 'The World at One'. It was not started on the basis of data analysis, focus groups or anything else; just the specialists' instinct of Mansell and Hardcastle that this was the right thing to do. Thirty years on, it looks a pretty good editorial call. Research and marketing had very little to do with its creation and nothing to do with its success.

So marketing and the arts have a problem. Let us pose the antitheses in a stark way: unfair perhaps, extreme undoubtedly, but not illegitimate.

Art is adventurous, marketing safe; art seeks the unexpected, marketing yearns for the predictable; art wants the amazing, marketing the comfortable; art is orgasmic, marketing anal. Yet we need both, and we both want to make money; we both want the biggest audiences. We have no alternative but to live together, and to live together in a constructive way, learning from and understanding one another.

And the list of things that the arts want from marketing is huge. Can marketing live up to the challenge? Why is it better at saying what the audience does not like rather than the circumstances under which it might embrace the unfamiliar? Why is it not better at constructing the case against charges of elitism in the arts, especially when they are nonsense? Why is it not better at achieving for the arts the breakthrough to the new wider audience?

The truth is that the arts need to know much more about marketing than they do. They must as a matter of course become proficient in business planning, press and publicity, design and production, and, yes, marketing. But each of these is no more than an essential tool for realising the basic artistic idea, the creative vision. Unless the arts master them, these skills will master the arts and distort them, preventing them from doing what they want to do. These techniques, too, must become part of our arts credo.

For I know that the arts will continue to be underfunded; I know that those who work in them will be underpaid; I know that those who participate do so out of love; I know that those who create do so out of belief. I also know that a society without the arts will be a spiritual desert. In such a Hell, I know that no amount of marketing will convince anyone that it is really Heaven. And I know for sure that if the arts do not help themselves, no one else will.

So, I do believe in the bottom line; I am committed to vision and mission statements; I am driven by objectives; I am devoted to the box office. I believe in marketing, too. Because I believe in the arts first.

11 The Concert of the Future – Seeing Will Be Hearing

In 1996, the *Daily Telegraph*'s music columnist, Norman Lebrecht, pronounced the imminent death of the classical music concert. The sickly patient's decline had, according to this obituary, been brought on by a combination of financial greed on the part of musicians and their agents, the reduction in state and corporate funding and a terminal weakening of the public's 'concert habit'.

Three years on, it is worth re-examining Lebrecht's prognosis, trying to establish whether it was a well-judged or exaggerated storm warning, or whether it was all too realistically flying the white flag of surrender over several centuries of musical culture. If the latter, then it is time to write a long, sad postscript to an experience of live performance that might be summed up as lasting from Mantua and Mannheim to the Concertgebouw and the Royal Albert Hall.

If the classical concert truly is dead, or at best just breathing out its dying gasp, then it will be farewell to the sight and sound of the Brendels, the Kissins, the Schiffs, the Perahias, the Pollinis and their like; to the Sterns, the Mutters, the Chungs, the Changs, the Vengerovs, to Yo-Yo and Slava, to Valery and Seiji, to Claudio and Bernard, to Zubin and Colin and all the performers who have lit up concert hall platforms and the lives of their audiences for a generation.

Put as starkly as that, are existing concert-lovers likely to abandon these artists and the experience of hearing them live so readily? I doubt it. Come to that, are the generations of still-to-be-created or converted concert-goers ready to forego or to be excluded from such riches of experience of performance and music? I doubt that too, but that is a belief rather than a provable assertion.

Besides, the current experience suggests that, despite difficulties, concert-going in all its varied forms is still alive and kicking. The BBC Promenade Concerts – now globally branded and recognised as the 'BBC Proms' – have successfully transmuted themselves from being a 'mere' music festival – albeit the largest and most varied in the world – into an extension of the British summer season, an event to attend and to be seen at, an occasion for corporate hospitality, a desirable 'positional good'. People who probably go to no other concert in the year go to a Prom because it has become an extension of the 'things to do' in the summer. But first and foremost, when they go to a Prom, the audience goes to a concert, and they go in their tens of thousands.

Skilfully promoted, the Proms have not changed their musical character at the behest of the needs of marketing. They had become a musical landmark, national and international, in their own right well before they became an 'occasion', as a result of sticking to their basic belief in the provision of an increasingly broad and eclectic musical repertoire played to the highest standards. The sense that a visit to a Prom is part of the traditional experience of concert-going does not inhibit people from attending some, indeed, like it better for the very fact that 'it's traditional'. Yet, elsewhere and at other times, the sheer act of taking part in a conventional performance where the audience sits in silence and the musicians dress in white tie and tails, is said to represent a barrier for those who are not regular visitors. They feel 'excluded' by the unfamiliarity of the event and the occasion.

Of course, not all concerts are full all the time. But it does not follow that because many are less well-attended than they deserve to be, the experience of going to concerts is being fundamentally rejected or will inevitably have to be abandoned.

Yet to debate like this is essentially sterile and backward-looking. It would be extraordinary if a way of enjoying the public performance of music that has been set for a century or more should not change, change radically, and change for the better. There is a debate to be had about the form and presentation of the concert – more or less classical – and it is a forward-looking debate that centres on how artists and performers relate to the audience and, more fundamentally, to the use and adaptation of current technology. Used properly, thoroughly and imaginatively, technology could transform the concert-going experience, and benefit significantly the economics of providing classical music.

But first, how do you connect the artists more closely to the live listeners? How do you close the gap between those on the platform and those in the body of the hall? When the great Canadian jazz-pianist Oscar Peterson came to the Barbican in 1996, the concert began with the hall darkened, the stage empty, and spotlights on the awaiting array of music stands, instruments, chairs and piano. Then a voice on the loudspeaker system asked the audience to welcome the drummer, who walked on to a round of applause. The entire six man band was introduced in this way. As serious performers, it was right to identify them and right for them to be acknowledged individually. But their arrival also served as a steady build-up to the thunderous climax for the arrival of the man himself, Oscar Peterson. He was welcomed as the star of the evening but also as a star surrounded by a constellation whose contributions would be essential to the whole performance. There was something both dramatic and democratic about this walk-on routine. It created the atmosphere; we were part of an occasion.

Imagine a similar practice applied to a symphony orchestra. It could work like this. First, the bulk of the orchestra would walk on to the platform, with an appropriate public announcement of welcome, perhaps referring either to a recent overseas visit or to a recent success elsewhere in the country. After all, distinguished visiting orchestras are habitually applauded on to the platform. Why inhibit the warmth of the response for the home team just because they are familiar? The orchestra's section leaders would then arrive individually or in a group, with their names and the instruments they play being publicly announced. The orchestra's leader would still have the penultimate solo entrance, anticipating the climactic arrival of the conductor.

Such an introduction would personalise the orchestra's players, many of them soloists in their own right, give them added status and respect, and vastly increase the extent to which the audience could identify, and identify with, the musicians who play the instruments and make the sounds. It would reduce the gap between performers and listeners; it would lower some of the false barriers without diminishing respect for the activity.

Of course, most orchestras – and no doubt some in the audience – would hate it. It took Clive Gillinson, the LSO's Managing Director, some time to persuade his band simply to turn and face the audience when they took their applause. As a gesture, this is simple and attractive. We want to applaud them as well as the conductor and soloist. We want to see their faces as well as their profiles, to relate to the orchestra whose skills and verve have just moved or excited us. We want the obstruction of the raised platform, the sense of them and us, the active and the passive, lessened even if they can never be wholly eliminated.

But behaving like this also encourages the orchestra to acknowledge the existence of the audience, thus establishing another part of the chain of recognition and reaction that could strengthen and give warmth to the concert experience. Using this suggested 'arrival sequence' would hugely enhance the sense of sharing and immediacy in the concert hall. It would be a small, immediate, practical step to reduce some of the sense of anxiety or bewilderment that the occasional concert goer faces. Faces would be put together with names; names with instruments; instruments could then be more easily connected with the sounds heard.

But a further step in this process is needed, one which embraces the latest in current electronic technology. With the use of television cameras, the entire evening could be transformed and enhanced in a revolutionary way. Once the TV cameras are installed, the video captured by them can be used in ways that strengthen the whole practice, experience and public acceptance of concert-going.

Modern electronic technology has developed very fast. Cameras are smaller, lighter, less obtrusive, capable of remote operation and can operate on low lighting levels. In other words, bulky equipment, intrusive artificial lights, high staff costs from using manned cameras, are obsolete; so are the old high-capital outlays on the basic camera and TV gallery installations. The price for a fully rigged and crewed TV facility to provide image quality up to the standards demanded by the main terrestrial TV channels (BBC1 and 2, ITV and Channels 4 and 5) used to run at some £40,000 per hour. The sum per hour for programming a lightweight TV unit to deliver images suitable for one of the new digital channels has fallen to an attractively affordable £6,000.

Before examining the wider uses to which medium quality video transmission or recording could be put on TV channels, the impact of such a facility within the concert hall is worth a thought. Imagine the concert platform configured in such a way that, say, three large, high definition TV screens are built into the fabric of the building, taking into account the acoustic effects of the screen surfaces. Imagine, too, six fixed camera positions for the latest small, lightweight, high definition, unmanned, remote-controlled cameras. Remember, that this will be a hall using only the normal house lighting with no added glare or heat from serried banks of filming lights. The TV presence will be completely inconspicuous.

As result, the transmission, presentation elsewhere in the building, or the video recording of a concert can be done cheaply and without any specific, additional disturbance for performers or audience. It will be part of everyday life, a normal facility, a virtually automatic part of the concert scene – but a huge addition to its interests and pleasures.

The programming of the time surrounding any concert will be fuller, more complete intellectually, more varied visually and will present in the most accessible way to the listener the whole experience of participating in a concert. The aim is to add more information and enrichment to the primary activity of listening to the music. In the following suggested schedule, everything that appears on the TV screens in the hall is also available on screens in the foyers and in a relay room nearby. Naturally, everything is captured on video as well.

The 'Concert of the Future' could be presented like this. From 7 p.m., TV screens carry live a fifteen-minute introductory talk or interview with a performer which takes place on the concert platform. From 7.15, they show a five to ten minute promo about the orchestra, a recent tour, the artists, or material about future events in the hall. This stops five minutes before the concert starts as the audience finishes entering and settles down in their seats.

At 7.30, the orchestra enters, in the way described earlier, with voiced-over introductions and identification by name and instrument. The key orchestral section leaders and leader can be seen in close-up on screen as they take their places in the body of the orchestra. Throughout the performance, the main camera at the back of the platform is fixed on the conductor. How extraordinary that audiences pay tens of pounds to see Maestro X conduct and all they see during the concert is his backside. Using cameras and screens, they would see his face and gestures as they have never been seen by the audience before – as the orchestra or chorus see him. It represents a huge quantity of added value, access and education provided by one technical means.

During the concert, the three screens on stage offer a basic selection of shots to illustrate the music being played. It is not a question of attempting to replicate in the concert hall the complexity of images which are delivered to the home TV set the concert hall listener does not need them and would find them a distraction. The on-stage screens would pick out orchestral soloists, when it was helpful to know where sounds were coming from – not always easy even for an experienced concert-listener. They would clarify the action on the platform by showing the audience things they might not see otherwise; by drawing attention, for example, to a new theme or to an old one being taken up by different instruments. This additional visual information would remove any idea that there are arcane secrets about who is doing what among a hundred identically-suited

players. It would increase understanding of the work in performance and intensify pleasure in the music.

Imagine watching the LSO's principal timpanist, Kurt-Hans
Goedicke, subtly, almost inaudibly, impacting his timpani at the
start of Sibelius' First Symphony. Imagine watching the orchestra's cor anglais player, Christine Pendrill, breathing out the fate
theme in *Carmen*. These are the kinds of intimate moments –
there would be countless others – that live TV cameras could
open up to a hall audience, and which are only incidentally
viewable now by even experienced concert-goers. At the very
start of the performance, the screens could show the first page of
the orchestral score, offering a subtle reminder that the music is
about to start and encouraging even restless audiences to settle
more quickly. (You could have smaller screens in particular parts
of the hall carrying the entire musical score for those who want
to follow it but do not want to rustle pages and irritate their
neighbours.)

At the interval, with the orchestra off-stage and the audience
having a drink and stretching their legs, the screen presentation
would continue. For those who stayed in their seats (and there
are always some) the possibilities would be endless. There could
be audience interviews in the foyers with reactions to and
discussion of the first half of the concert, live discussion on the
platform about the second half by the composer, critics, players.
It would also offer the orchestra and the venue another
opportunity to trail forthcoming events, special offers or other
marketing opportunities. Then, after a simplified platform
routine for the orchestra's return, more music enhanced by TV
presentation.

There would of course be objections from some members of
the audience about this style of presentation. There always are.
For many, not unreasonably, the visual elements would seem,
and would be, a distraction. Using them would not be obligatory
at every concert; some orchestras or performers might decide to
shun such an atmosphere altogether. But there were objections
to surtitles in opera houses for a while until the great majority of
the audience made it clear that this technical facility enhanced

their artistic enjoyment hugely. The absence of surtitles would be inconceivable today.

I believe that, over time, the attractiveness of the experience to newcomers would more than outweigh any loss of support from established patrons – who could, anyway, learn to ignore the images. It would be a disaster if the existing audience were so alienated that it abandoned the concert hall while the new audience was not sufficiently persuaded to be convinced. But the experiment, or something like it, must surely be put to the test, to see where the tolerances or intolerances exist on both sides.

Such a proposed concert-hall configuration is not inimical to the spirit of the traditional concert; it involves no talking down, no leaning over backwards to pretend that a concert is different from what it actually is; it invites nobody to become artistic mutton dressed up as populist lamb. It does not sell the music, the performers or the occasion short. It offers no false prospectuses about what is going on.

But there is even more to this proposal than clarifying and enhancing the experience of a night in the concert hall. Once the TV equipment is installed, the images captured can be used in a variety of different ways for no extra price. For a start, the sequence of events set out above could be transmitted live to a TV channel, with a minimum of ancillary commentary and perhaps some few extra visual ingredients. While the comparatively restricted technical quality of the pictures might militate against their transmission on a mainstream terrestrial network, they are fully adequate, in terms of cost and quality, for one of the new digital channels.

The importance of such a development can hardly be overstated. Top quality arts performances on video are in desperately short supply in relation to the amount of channel air-time now becoming obtainable in the new digital packages. The arts must have their place in tomorrow's myriad proliferation of TV channels, preferably on more than one such outlet. Technology now permits the performing arts to be as available as sport or other entertainment. Cost is ceasing to be a barrier to presenting our arts wares to as wide a public as possible – and might even make them as popular. Tuning in to an arts channel could be as regular and frequent as switching on any other – except, perhaps, football. It is potentially the biggest widening of access to both existing and new audiences in the history of the arts.

Furthermore the recorded video, whether used for TV transmission or not, then exists as a happy memento to be mulled over at leisure or as an educational instrument. Schools, hospitals, music groups, supporters clubs would be hugely enriched by the steady availability of once-fleeting performances now captured on tape. For the orchestra, too, the ownership of this recorded body of performances would represent the start of the accumulation of a capital base of what can rightly be described as 'product' – something more to show for all those hours of rehearsal and the strain of a concert, and to sell.

Beyond such practical advantages, whether you like it or not the presence and involvement of television increasingly confers a sort of legitimacy on events. To exclude the performing arts from it would be to imply that they were excluding themselves from public esteem. That would undermine the case for continuing public subsidy and bring nearer the death of the performing arts. As I watch the numerous TV sports programmes with football players and managers floundering to say something interesting with a handful of repetitive clichés, I fantasise about a classical music equivalent. The post-concert interview in the Green Room would go like this:

Interviewer: 'Well, Clive, how did it go tonight?'

Manager: 'I thought the boys and girls played a blinder. The team work was wonderful, the attack was overwhelming, and there was no doubt who came out on top – it was Beethoven.'

Interviewer: 'What pleased you most about the playing tonight?'

Manager: 'Well, I liked the way the themes were distributed so unselfishly. No one held onto them too long, each section picked the theme up and ran

	with it, and it had tremendous drive and passion.'
Interviewer:	'Any particular stars tonight?'
Manager:	'Well, you've got to single out Andrew Marriner – what a great clarinettist. And of the young stars, well David Pyatt has got to be the best first horn in any British Orchestra.'

Who could say that such conversations – and such a channel – would not be far more rewarding and real than their football equivalents?

But caution is needed; we should not be over-optimistic. In the recent past new forms of technological delivery of music have not increased concert-going audiences. Very often, they may have created a beguiling and convenient substitute for that activity. Opera-lovers listen to opera on hi-fi CDs rather than travelling, paying and sitting. Even the video of an opera pays off its cost at a single sitting – it is, after all, much less than the price of a single seat. No amount of urging that there is no substitute for the real thing can by itself sweep aside economic realities. A night out is a single occasion; a CD or video can fill a score of evenings.

Furthermore, it is doubtful that the video would have the hoped for and vaunted *Nessun Dorma* or 'Three Tenors' effect, or the Classic FM factor. Surely, it was once argued, all those who thrilled to a few minutes of Pavarotti giving his all in the signature tune to Italia '90 would become instant converts to *Turandot* and then seamlessly convert to the whole world of opera as a result? If there were any who decided to see *Turandot* on the strength of the World Cup, my guess is that they would have fidgeted before the Big Number came, then been appalled by how long the work dragged on after it, with no reprise to cheer them up.

The fact is that opera is not like dipping into a box of chocolates. It is demanding, difficult; it needs concentration and must be taken on its own terms. This does not make it elitist, it merely restates the awkward fact that those very experiences that are worthwhile are not easily mastered. Most of the great moments in opera, notably those celebrated 'bleeding hunks' of Wagner, are greater in their true context than when removed from it. Of course, Siegfried's funeral music in the hands of a Toscanini or Tennstedt makes an unforgettable impact even when played in isolation. But its effect in its right place, at the end of four operas and some fifteen hours of music is far, far greater. Conversely, there are a goodly number of operas – such as Bizet's *Pearl Fishers* – where the big number really is just that, and the rest is something of a come-down. One spectacular piece of operatic exposure on television does not remove obstacles or guarantee access. The whole process is more complex than that.

Similarly, the failure of the expected Classic FM factor provides a salutary warning against facile optimism. Many assumed or hoped that the sheer availability of short works or extracts from the great classics, of a limited, familiar and predictable play-list, would whet the appetite of listeners for more and they would trade up from the gobbet of the opera or single movement of the symphony to the whole work and the real thing. Undoubtedly there are some who do, but on the whole the 'trickle up' of classical music listening has proved as elusive and unreal as the much vaunted 'trickle down' factor in free market economics: make the rich richer and their wealth will trickle down to those they employ and the things they buy. Neither has worked and in the case of classical music it has not worked for a simple reason.

Those who listen to Classic FM are not doing so because they regard the station as a painless ante-chamber to Radio 3. They listen to Classic FM because that is what they want. They do not want and may not like whole symphonies or operas or string quartets. They are quite content with fragments, extracts and easy listening. They are not especially curious about what they do not know. This is mood listening not serious listening, something different not something worse. The hope that these listeners would migrate painlessly, willingly and in considerable numbers to Radio 3 was naive to start with and has proved vain.

These chastening examples of failed breakthroughs in popularising classical music might suggest that the 'TV in the Concert Hall' idea is bound to end with more disappointment and disillusionment for those of us dedicated to widening and deepening the base of classical music-lovers. I do not believe that it will.

My radical scenario takes the classical concert as it is and integrates television with it in such a way that it opens the doors of the concert hall physically and symbolically. It removes anxiety about the apparently private rituals of the concert, it adds accessible communication about the event in such a way that the performance and the performers are demystified. It will never fully 'explain' a piece of music, it will never make a new work simple. But even the sight and sound of composers – such as James MacMillan, Michael Berkeley, Tom Ades or George Benjamin – talking about their work before a concert might reassure the listener that a composer is a human being, who happens to have exceptional sensibilities and spends his or her life trying to do something desperately difficult but splendidly selfless: communicating human emotion through the organisation of sound.

In November 1998, the Barbican presented a 90th Birthday Concert tribute to the great American composer Elliott Carter. No one would pretend that Carter's music, including the long, fifty-minute work premiered on this occasion, *Symphonia*, is anything but intellectually stretching and complex to the ear and mind. The evening was transformed by introducing that and the two chamber music works in the first half with some five to six minutes of video of Carter talking about his pieces and finally engaging in lively conversation with Pierre Boulez about the rights and wrongs of a conductor ignoring a composer's own markings. The combination of the video and the music produced a very different feel to the evening than the music played alone.

But the clinching strategic argument for going down the road I have sketched out is the absolute need for classical music in performance to regain its place in the universe of the electronic media. The decline of classical music on BBC TV – a few Proms apart – has been as disastrous for classical music as it has been indefensible for the BBC. Music in performance must become a normal part of what the multi-channel viewers have on offer on their screens. Music cannot force its way onto them. But concerts must do everything that they can to remove the barriers – institutional, organisational, attitudinal – that prevent such a process. There is a price to be paid for making this new concert-hall environment possible, the price of entirely new flexibility on the part of musicians and soloists. If the orchestras do not make themselves available by helping to create that environment, then the ultimate price to be paid, of a weakening public awareness of the existence of classical music at all, will be huge.

12 The Cart and the Horse – Which Came First: The Market or the Art?

Imagine that you are the director of an arts centre or arts institution. Imagine that you are having a disappointing season at the box office. Imagine that your grant – if you have one – is being cut. Imagine that your sponsorship targets are contracting. What is your reaction? Call in the marketing department and blame them for not selling the tickets? Ask the press department why they are getting so few feature articles about your work? Quiz the education department about why the next generation audience for the arts has not appeared yet? Demand of the house manager why the atmosphere in your centre is so unfriendly and off-putting? Summon the catering concessionaire and insist that the bar staff are more friendly?

Show me the arts director or administrator who swears he or she has not responded to financial difficulties by doing one or all of these things and I will show you a liar. I go further. If you habitually resort to more than one of these, you should not be an arts director or manager. 'The fault dear Brutus lies in ourselves, not in our stars.' The fault, dear colleagues, lies in our arts policies not in the services that surround them.

If things are going wrong at an arts centre, then the strategy is wrong. No amount of press articles, good customer care, corporate sponsorship, educational outreach, or niche marketing can, of themselves, save you. None of these activities should be blamed. There is an old Czech saying about managerial responsibility: 'A fish stinks from the head.' Arts managers and directors are at the head of their organisations. If there is a bad smell, don't look accusingly at somebody else; check your own halitosis.

I put my case rather earthily, because I think we are in danger of being buried under loads of managerial cant about business and business methods that distracts from the essential, the first task, of having an artistic policy of which audiences want to be a part. Everything else is secondary – from selling seats, to making audiences feel welcomed, to catering for whatever their food and drink tastes may be. All these are necessary conditions for success; but they will not in themselves create a thriving and vigorous arts centre.

The one and only sufficient cause for excellence and success in the arts is the artistic policy itself. As the former Director of the BBC Proms Sir John Drummond once said, memorably: 'It's the marketing department's job to sell what the artistic director decides.' What I am talking about is balance, proportion and priorities, not about whether marketing is valuable. Of course it is. But how must it be used to make it as effective as it needs to be?

Let us take the argument one stage further. Imagine an arts centre where public transport drops audiences off at the front door and picks them up at curtain-down without fail; where the car parks are never full and there are no queues as cars leave; where the food is delicious and cheap, the surroundings and architecture spacious and welcoming, the programmes beautifully laid out, the season discounts tempting beyond the dreams of avarice, and every usher smiles and wishes you an enjoyable evening – imagine a place, in short, where 'every prospect pleases and only the art is indifferent'.

Of course, that would not be enough. It is not a ridiculous scenario; it has its attractions; but ultimately it would be a fairly pointless one. The relationship between the service functions and the main arts activity cannot work that way. Marketing the tickets – or press, or customer care – cannot make up for the shortcomings of the arts policies themselves. Only art can produce miracles; and marketing does not need to sell them, they sell themselves. So what can and should marketing do for the arts? What can it not do for the arts?

For a start, marketing and market research cannot devise an

arts strategy, because none of us – as audiences – really know what we want, and most of us are sufficiently mature to take a risk with the unfamiliar if we trust the arts policy overall. Audiences often only like what they hear once they have been attracted by it through publicity and tasted it for themselves. Persuasion and information play their part; but they must have some message to transmit.

Like it or not, arts programming is best left as the preserve of the inspired, benevolent autocrat. History – past and recent – is littered with examples that bear this out. No prior marketing research told Clive Gillinson, the Managing Director of the London Symphony Orchestra, to mount a huge cycle of all fifteen of the Shostakovich symphonies in 1998. (Indeed, at least one music critic told him that it was wrong to do so as an artistic policy.) A brave manager might have mounted a cycle of the symphonies from Number Five onwards, drawing a deep breath as he did so. But in the event, Gillinson, Mstislav Rostropovich, the conductor, and the LSO, were rewarded with big houses for the risk they took, and added recognition from the critics that at least three of the previously rarely played early symphonies were worth taking seriously.

No focus group told the BBC to devote an entire weekend of seven concerts to the work of the Czech nationalist Bohuslav Martinu in 1998, or of eight great concerts to the great French Catholic visionary Olivier Messiaen in 1999. Nicholas Kenyon, then Radio 3 Controller, decided that the time was ripe for a longer, considered hearing of these composers' output, and he had his reward with good houses, excellent reviews and some memorable broadcasts.

Good market research can point in broad directions, can suggest lines of approach, can warn of likely dangers, can interpret matters of style, presentation and image. But it cannot tell the arts director what to do. Focus groups without number cannot answer the basic questions of 'what should you put on to the stage, the platform, or the screen'. They are too small and too personal to tell you much beyond what the handful of people involved feel at the time. They are a poor guide to considered decisions or to likely future behaviour. Atmospheric they may be, well-meaning they undoubtedly are, but they require heavy filtering through the protecting veil of common sense.

The comments of focus groups invite us to lend far too much weight to the individual observations of the members. After the Martinu Weekend at the Barbican, one enthusiastic member of the audience came up to me and said: 'Thank you for such a wonderful weekend. Now please can we have one devoted to Josef Suk?' Another said, 'Well, I know he is overshadowed by Tchaikovsky, but what a treat a weekend of Glazunov would be.' Even experts can get it wrong. One well-known international conductor, after a successful weekend of concerts by Sibelius, said to me: 'You know what we should do next? All the symphonies of Berwald.' I love all three of the composers referred to – Suk, Glazunov, Berwald – but I can think of few easier ways of emptying halls or undermining artistic budgets.

It follows from this that the experience of marketing cannot plan your future programmes for you. Past box office is a poor predictor of future success. Take the task of composing the repertoire of an opera house. Perhaps *La Bohème* was a best-seller last year, as were *Madam Butterfly*, *Aida*, *Pearl Fishers* and *Carmen*. But if they are programmed again and again, or if they are given too long a run in any one season, the harsh reality is that audiences tail away. In our parents' time, the format of overture, concerto and symphony satisfactorily packed out concert hall after concert hall. The answer to concert planning appeared to be: 'Play them again, Sam.' Until that market collapsed too.

For marketing cannot tell artistic planners where to turn next. It did not predict the popularity of Mahler and Bruckner, the former surely now on the verge of over-exposure. The business of discovering that there was a huge audience for the very late romantics was ground out by hard graft, artistic hunch, and commercial daring.

On the other hand, marketing and targeting can successfully maximise a small audience for specialist performers or repertoire of works of minority taste. Some kinds of marketing are excellent at delivering niche audiences for niche products, and for building the core of the audience. I do not believe though that marketing alone ever delivers the full house. That universally longed-for sight comes from a combination of factors, including word of mouth and a sense of occasion, qualities that defy analysis, that defy prediction and that defy the rules of salesmanship. To reach the happy moment when audience demand exceeds the supply of tickets also depends on that special mix of the right programme and artistes, the right advance press, publicity and pricing, and the right marketing. But all the ingredients in the recipe need to be in place. One is not enough by itself.

What else can marketing not do? When it addresses the strategic questions of shaping a new branding policy for a centre, it cannot by itself make an arts institution – whether theatre, concert hall, or orchestra – loved, admired or respected. No amount of changing names, conceptualising logos, designing letterheads, formulating marketing slogans out of mission statements, or other exercises in corporate branding, can give an arts centre a profile unless the institution itself has a real personality. Subsequent marketing and branding activities can raise the profile of the place once it has earned one but it cannot fabricate one where none exists. Only an arts policy can do that.

The reward is to be found when these activities work hand in hand. The Barbican's decision to invest a great deal of time, money and creative effort in a year-long American season called 'Inventing America' in 1998, was primarily an artistic decision. But the way that the idea, those programmes, those artists were knitted into a coherent and captivating set of images and slogans was an object lesson in the effectiveness of strong marketing building on a strong creative theme.

That partnership added a further benefit to what turned out to be a successful season. It was also – though it was not planned for that purpose – a significant step in re-branding the image of the Barbican Centre itself by declaring a strong association between high artistic quality, an immensely varied programme, and a bright, confident image. The fact that festival after festival elsewhere in Britain later discovered the American theme showed that we had caught something in the air before others did.

Marketing cannot substitute for artistic conviction or thought. Like any other management tool, it must be the servant of the core activity – arts. If it is not controlled, unbridled reliance on marketing – or on any other management device – becomes like the sorcerer's apprentice going on and on without rhyme or reason, ultimately defeating the whole purpose of the exercise. An arts director who loses control of marketing and its strategy has lost control of the institution.

These reservations are necessary because the idea is afoot in many quarters that 'if only the arts could market themselves properly, then they would not need to ask for so much money'. If only it were that simple. So what can marketing do to maximise the audience, to ensure that the best devised programming gets the public it deserves? Only a fool would not use every management means in his power to make the arts institution as effective as possible. First the music, then the words; first the policy, then its delivery. How should they fit together?

It is axiomatic that every arts institution should be as professional and expert in all areas of activity as it is possible to be. There is no room for excuses or evasion when it comes to financial disciplines and controls, budget setting, maximisation of secondary sales, commercial exploitation. We do not need outside financial experts to do it for us; we must do it for ourselves.

There are many questions to which the arts world needs to know the answers, or at least about which it needs more information. For instance, research and marketing should be addressing some or all of the following: why do so many members of the audience come once a year only? Is it all they can afford? Is it all they have time for? Is the annual visit to the theatre or a concert like the annual Christmas visit to church? Do they come once and so fail to enjoy it that they never return? Is the performing arts audience made up of a comparatively small nucleus of the professionally-committed and a much larger group of casual visitors which churns between attendance and non-attendance?

The impact of turning each one-time visitor into a second-time visitor on a regular basis would be huge. It would be extremely economical as well. How do we do it? What information do we need to do it? It is often said that turning the single visitor into a serial participant is the key task facing arts institutions. By comparison, winning each new first-time attender is dismissed as being uneconomically expensive.

Well, so it may be. But something about the assumptions behind that revolts my spirit. We are being invited to pull up the drawbridge behind a fairly small gathering of the faithful and to decide that that is all we can afford to do. I think that is miserably defensive. We cannot exist without going out and trying to get the new audience members as well as reinforcing the habits of those already won over. Surely our aim must be to increase the overall pool of attenders as well as increasing the frequency of their visits.

Much is made these days of the idea of exclusion – that is to say, the notion that there is some kind of barrier of taste, knowledge or behaviour connected with the arts that is almost designed to keep out the well-intentioned but uninitiated. My first reaction to someone who says that some activity is too difficult – whether in the arts or in sport – is to reply, 'How hard have you tried yourself?' I would not go as far as Pierre Boulez who replied when asked about audiences' continuing terror of twentieth-century music: 'In my opinion it is laziness. They are not in the habit of listening and do not want to acquire the habit.' Then he added as a comment on those who want entertainment rather than searching art: 'It's like saying that you admire a mountain landscape but then finding that climbing one of those mountains is quite hard. There's no escape from the fact that anything worthwhile may also be a struggle.'

How many arts institutions are prepared to blazon on our mission statements a Government Health Warning: 'Visiting an Arts Institution May Make your Mind Hurt.' How, therefore, can all our best research find ways of bringing appeal to the essential fact that living art is not something cosy and comfortable, but challenging and often disturbing.

When questions of the failure to attract large audiences come up, much is made of the danger that current education policies – in Britain at least – are so geared to passing on information about the present that they ignore the accumulated knowledge of the past. Audiences of the future are not being created by the schools which put such a heavily contemporary focus onto learning and claim that unless something is 'relevant' to children and the world they know, then it will not be learned and therefore should not be taught.

Is it true that the next generation is being disabled from taking part in the arts because of lack of formal education in them – particularly music teaching – and sheer lack of information? It sometimes looks as if the audience of the future is a lost generation, rather like Peter Pan's Lost Boys. But we need more information about the extent of the loss and a better strategy for putting it right.

More important, though, is the campaign that is still being fought by the arts world, with increasing success, to persuade governments that arts and music teaching is not an optional add-on to the curriculum but is an essential part of personal and social education. Marketing might help us here – but the prior role must be taken up by political advocacy and the engagement of the press in a vital public debate. The arts community must deploy every skill it possesses if it is to continue to flourish. Unless we speak up for ourselves and mobilise campaigns on behalf of the arts, no one will believe that we have a case worth taking seriously. Today, every arts manager and director must be a publicist and crusader too. Governments and arts administrators do not like it – they want a quiet life – but the arts gain nothing from behaving like lambs waiting for the slaughter.

The questions to which we need answers multiply. For instance, why are arts institutions – and the media in all their forms – urged to appeal to the youth market as if that market were going to dominate the pool from which we take our audiences? The demographic evidence from one of Britain's leading research firms – MORI – is exactly the opposite. The proportion of young people in the British population has fallen from 26% in 1971 to 20% in 1991 and will fall to 16% by 2021. Naturally, the proportion of the population in the grey or greying category is growing proportionately, and it is precisely the educated and reasonably well-off members of the 'third age' category who are increasing. Haven't people always turned to the more serious arts as they mature? From this pattern, which applies to Europe as a whole the conclusion for the arts world ought to be that its potential audience is on the increase. Why has this part of the analysis been ignored? If we persist in drawing up arts policies overwhelmingly aimed at the youth audience when the population overall is ageing, then we risk skewing our activities and priorities in a quite disastrous way. No one wants concert halls to be filled only with the middle-class, the middle-aged and the comparatively well-off. But they are a potential audience who should not be disregarded in the pursuit of the young. Why are the middle-aged and the middle-class the only segments of society that have no right to protest at exclusion? There are signs that newspapers and TV stations are at least starting to question their own headlong and so far uncritical 'rush to youth'.

It is also often asserted that audiences for classical music are falling, according to some that they are in terminal decline. They are certainly more diverse, more specialised in their interests, and spread over a hugely increased number of performances and venues. Put together the figures for festivals that fill the land each spring and summer, for national and regional orchestras giving performances, and international orchestras visiting, add in the stubborn persistence of London in supporting no fewer than five major orchestras and a vast proliferation of new ensembles, and it is hard to believe that the overall total of those attending classical music performances is falling. Fundamental demand may well be buoyant; but it could have splintered into many more tastes and forms. If this is correct, then competition from differentiated venues and performers is our problem, rather than a lack of interest. Responding to the correct symptom is crucial.

The remedy will be different in each case. But we are invited to behave and act – as if the research points to one conclusion only – a fall in demand.

There is anecdotal evidence to back my scepticism and to suggest that it is possible to increase supply and to create demand. Take the Wigmore Hall in London, now recognised as the world's most successful chamber-music and song-recital venue. A generation back, the hall was closed on Sunday evenings and even some weekday nights because the audience – country-home-owning, well-to-do – was simply not there. Today, the 'Sunday Morning Coffee' concerts are sell-outs, and the Sunday evening concerts are just as likely to sell out as the others. The reason is that the audience for such music has not only changed but grown hugely. I do not believe that the Wigmore Hall is the only institution to buck the supposed trend. The Wigmore, under the single-minded artistic direction of William Lyne, has achieved its present eminence, a high point in its hundred-year history, since adopting an uncompromising policy of putting artistic quality first. Its reputation has sprung from its artistic actions. Artistic and financial success have followed. Thereafter, marketing this success, boosting ticket-sales and getting the message to the press were relatively easy. Today, its seemingly effortless association with artistic excellence makes the subsequent needs of branding and positioning easy.

In 1995, the Barbican Centre faced an awkward dilemma when the Royal Shakespeare Company announced its withdrawal from the Centre for six months each year. Some thought it insoluble. We could have washed our hands of the problem and decided it was too difficult to find a substitute for the RSC. Or we could have handed over to a commercial management to fill the gap. Instead – with further support from our funders, the Corporation of London – we reshaped the theatre into a fully flexible performance space. Backed by Arts Director Graham Sheffield's artistic hunch and supported by market research, a programme of international drama, dance and lyric theatre was assembled, unique in London since the celebrated Peter Daubeny

Seasons of International Theatre a generation ago. The Barbican's 'BITE '98' season was a fruitful combination of artistic belief and market research. It was high-risk. It was experimental. It was good quality. It was very expensive. Artistically, it was the only real option for the Centre if it wanted to advance from the situation that it was in. The task of marketing was to present that season not only to meet our box-office targets, but to persuade audiences to come because they understood the relationship between the centre, the events it was presenting, and the standards at which they were offered.

We did not meet our box-office targets. That was not a reflection on marketing but on a very ambitious set of artistic decisions. If there was a budget penalty for our ambition to be paid, we knew why we were paying it. There were alternative rewards. Not least among them was that the season reinforced the process of repositioning the Centre and re-branding it. Long seen as an essentially 'classical arts' centre, it began to be recognised as an institution with commitment to the classical-arts canon at its core; but with a knowledge of the contemporary arts scene in all the diversity of its forms as an essential part of its character.

This process will be taken on in a systematic way in due course. Here, the marketing professionals will play their part in interpreting and presenting to the public in a defined way the manner in which this particular centre has changed and developed. It is not so much that the artistic horse must come before the marketing cart; it is a fact that unless they pull together and in the same direction, neither of them will get anywhere.

13 The A-to-Z of Running an Arts Centre

I f anyone asks whether running an arts institution is a hard job, be it an orchestra, a gallery, a museum, or something that embraces all these activities such as an arts centre, the only honest answer is to say that it is as easy as learning the alphabet – but a new fuller one. The time is long gone when running a concert hall was mainly about programming the music, heading a gallery was chiefly about the paintings on the walls, directing a theatre company was principally about that – directing plays.

Running the arts is more like a business than it ever used to be. In some respects, it is even more complex. On top of the routine financial disciplines that are demanded as a matter of course and necessity, arts organisations work in fields where forecasting audience-response to the artistic programme is notoriously difficult. Tastes change; taste can be shaped; taste needs be led. Predicting audience response to the artistic offering is hazardous. Eliminating risk is impossible; often the safe conservative line in artistic provision is the most risky. The middle of the road – whether in art or in walking – is the place where you are run over. Nothing is as old hat in the arts as last year's proven winners.

So, how is the basic question to be answered? Is running the arts difficult – that is to say as complex as a business – or is it really as easy as ABC? Perhaps reciting the alphabet will give us the answer to the question.

A is for Audiences and Access and Accountability and, yes, I almost forgot, the Arts. I put the word 'audiences' in the plural – there are dozens of distinct arts audiences, many separate ones for classical music alone. Sir John Drummond, when Controller of

BBC Radio 3 and Director of the Proms, always said that the Radio 3 listeners were composed of dozens of groups who passionately loved one kind of music and – more importantly – loathed the others. Yet, particular as their range of tastes may be, audiences are united by a shared enthusiasm for, and a common commitment to, the arts as a whole. That commitment distinguishes them from their fellow citizens who find no interest in or draw no comfort from artistic activity of any kind. It certainly does not make arts supporters better; it does mark them off as different.

Access is a comparatively new concern. It means more than finding your way around a building, though as I know from bitter experience at the Barbican, that is not a small issue. 'Access' has the precise connotation of extending the social range, the ethnic variety, the class cross-section of your audiences. The arts, we have been told, are exclusive, or at least are perceived as such. A slippery word, 'perceived'. It can lay any accusation against you without providing solid evidence for the charge. So, if anyone 'perceives' the arts as being exclusive, then they have no choice but to try to remove that (perceived) view. If audiences are kept out because they 'feel' excluded, then it is up to arts institutions to change that feeling. In actual fact, any worthwhile arts organisation is desperate to widen and deepen its audience base. Enabling access for each and every one is only a means to a common goal, that of more people coming to and enjoying the arts.

A is also for Accountability. To whom? To those who provide the money to fund the arts, for sure. It is good manners to say 'thank you' in any case, not to mention common sense. Currently, the word holds a somewhat technical meaning: that of answering for your actions to as wide a constituency of people and institutions as possible. To those who ask why you do what you do, you should not only have a good answer, but offer it without complaint or reservation. The call for accountability reflects a need for the arts to tell society more actively why they act as they do, why they spend as they do. It invites the arts to be more persuasive, more open about their beliefs, more bold in their justification, more ready to engage in debate, more eager to confront questioning.

And yes, A is for Arts. 'What is art?' as the questioning Pontius Pilate might have asked, and he would not have stayed for an answer to that question either. If my own answer is not clear by the end of this alphabet, then I have more than a letter missing.

B is for Box Office and Backstage and Business Plan. Take your box office, its head and the staff very seriously. The box office both sells the tickets, and sells the idea of the institution. Its staff represent the place over the phone, and even more so face-to-face. A mishandled phone enquiry can lose a sale in the first few seconds; should the call take minutes to be answered, it can be lost still more quickly. If you ring another venue's box office, you can tell instantly what that place is like. Seen like this, the box office is not only your public face but it proclaims how warm a heart you have.

Backstage are the staff who interact with your artists. Why should international or national stars return to your centre if the treatment they receive backstage is anything but expert, friendly and helpful? The staff may be 'backstage' to the audience but they are face-to-face for the artists. A Green Room which does not feel welcoming, worse, one which is positively off-putting, will make it difficult for artists to perform at their best. They could judge you and their whole experience not by the cheers of the audience but by the glowers of your backstage staff.

B is for Business Plan. The arts world is full of ideas. People like working in it because it thrives on ideas. Sorting out the good from the bad, the clever from the barmy, the original from the merely wacky, is tricky. One useful discipline is to insist on a business plan for any proposal. It will not tell you whether it is a good idea as such, but it will identify just how financially precarious it will be and it will certainly make it clear if you are likely to lose your shirt on it. (More about risk later.)

C is for Customers and Consumers and Communication and Commercial Activities. Oh and Catering, too. Are customers different from audiences? Well, you certainly want their 'custom'.

You always have. So, why change the noun? I do not know, but I have good grounds for being suspicious. Was it mere accident that when the railways changed from treating travellers as passengers to calling them 'customers', the service immediately got worse?

Those who come to the Barbican are certainly our customers. But when they go to a concert or watch a movie or go to the theatre, they have always been the audience, for the very good reason that they come here to listen. The word describes their attendance very precisely – they have come to listen, to attend, to participate. To reduce this rich, complex human activity – that of being an audience – to a mere commercial transaction – that of being a customer – is to diminish both the activity, the artists who provide it and the people who value it. (Of values, more later.)

Oddly enough, I mind the idea of 'consumers' far less. As audiences are to art, consumers are to entertainment. Come to that, I often say that I 'consume' art in the sense that I thrive on it. But if the act of consumption is less rich in a philosophical sense than the experience of being part of an audience ('consumption' after all has overtones of being more casual, less intense, less highly regarded), it still remains a more collective human pastime, usually devoted to shared enjoyment and therefore ranking some levels above the commercially reduced business of being regarded as a mere customer. So my own hierarchy of values runs, from the best to the less good: audience, consumer, customer.

C is for Communication. Telling your staff what you are doing, what the arts institution is doing, is an essential part of management. Either you communicate directly and openly, or the grapevine (at its best) or the rumour machine (at its worst) will do the job for you. Taking and keeping the initiative in the communication campaign is crucial for another reason. If management does not do it, the unions will do it for you. There is nothing wrong with the unions; but they transmit their message and not yours. But communication is a two-way process: it does not merely flow from the top down. There must be ways of having it flow back from staff to managers and management must show that it listens to what is being said.

C is for Commercial Activities. There is hardly an arts venue of any kind which does not sell its time, its space or its facilities to outside interests. We are all rooms for hire these days. But there is a great fantasy abroad: that you can fund the arts programmes by being sufficiently commercial in your exploitation of the buildings and facilities. This is an illusion. The Barbican was opened in 1982 on the confident assumption that its commercial activities would pay for the arts programming. Sixteen years on, the Corporation of London is still funding the centre to the extent of some £23 million a year in operating costs. Without our commercial activities – ranging from catering to car parks to retail to conferences and trade exhibitions – that subsidy would have to be still larger. So while they are a necessary part of the economy of an arts centre, they will never provide a sufficient source of finance to run one in its entirety on any scale.

And talking of which, a vital ingredient of these commercial activities is Catering. Like Napoleon's army, an arts institution marches on its stomach – or rather on everyone else's. Of course the notorious Victoria and Albert Museum advertising campaign that it was 'An Ace Caff with a Museum Attached', showed just how wrongly you can present a message. The museum or concert hall or theatre must always come first. But the fact is that catering does matter. Eating out is an increasing part of social life and for some people a principal form of entertainment. If arts venues do not provide food in a variety of settings and price levels, someone else will do it for them and pocket the profit. Retailers call it the 'Total Entertainment Offer'. We neglect it at our peril. The food which an institution provides tells the audience something about its values.

D is for Discounts and Disabled. The business of juggling with seat prices to attract more audiences is more than a commercial transaction, it has become an art. Judging the level at which the bargains are set, the time of week or day that the reductions are available, the frequency with which they are offered, can make a vast difference to your cash take and cash flow. Beware! Audiences have become extraordinarily canny and price-sensitive. The idea that arts audiences are all flush with cash is a shallow assumption based on broad ignorance of the people who really patronise the arts. They need to mind their pounds; they know what reductions are on offer and when they are available. They will hold off buying until the discounts kick in. Excessive discounting may fill the house, but it may empty the till at the same time.

D is for Disabled. Allowing the disabled to use the facilities as easily as if they had no disability is now an automatic expectation of any arts institution. From wheel-chair access, to convenient seats for those accompanying them, to induction loops for the hard-of-hearing, there is a long agenda of action points that have to be met before equality of provision can be claimed. The solutions are not only technical. Staff attitudes also determine whether the disabled feel a true part of the valued audience or just an inconvenience that must be accommodated. Are the disabled included in more than just a physical way? Awareness of their needs has grown faster than the ability of older buildings to adapt to them. The cost of adaptation is huge. The resources for it often do not exist. Sooner or later, the age and inflexibilities of a building will not be accepted as an excuse for sub-standard disabled provision. Reconciling the need with the inability to pay for it is a looming roadblock on the way ahead.

E is for Education and Excellence. Every arts institution should have its own education programme. Most do. They are not set up as a pleasant add-on; they are an integral part of the activity of opening up what the arts do to people of all ages who have had little opportunity to learn about or to experience them. Whether the education programme takes the basic art forms out to schools, or brings schools and groups into the building for a closer, more intimate involvement with the art in question, or whether the centre initiates arts activities with whole communities, the aim is the same. Education breaks down barriers, opens minds and doors, expands understanding and enjoyment. As much as anything else, it shows that the arts do not inhabit an ivory tower.

Two practical observations. Sponsors like educational projects; grant-giving bodies insist on them. One blunt truth. All the combined activities of every arts body in the country cannot make good the shortfall in the teaching and experience of the arts that the schools once gave but of which they provide less and less. One unpopular observation. An education programme in an arts institution cannot substitute for a part of the national schools budget. It is concerned with bringing audiences into the arts in larger numbers. Some arts education purists dispute this.

E is for Excellence. We are all supposed to be Centres of Excellence. To state that is to state the obvious. Who, after all, sets out to run a Centre of Mediocrity? At least the commitment to excellence signals to all that however experimental or occasionally esoteric arts activities may be from time to time – as distinct from being mainstream, conservative and predictable – they can be embraced as excellent on the grounds of their basic conception and intention or their realisation in performance.

F is for Front-of-House and Finance. Staff in the front-of-house (a good old-fashioned category) now dispense 'Customer Care' (a modish piece of managerial cant which is, however, so all-pervasive that it has to be used and cannot be ignored). Customer care began with the ubiquitous American restaurant farewell greeting of 'Have a Nice Day' – or 'afternoon' or 'evening' or 'late evening'. We have all laughed at it. But we are all used to it. When BA check-in clerks (or do I mean desk officers) call me by my name as they give me an upgrade, I feel better: I am an individual passenger rather than just another customer. An impersonal process has become personalised: we may be part of a vast transport sausage machine but we can at least feel that we have our own skin. The arts are not there to provide mass experiences in commercially compressed and packaged forms. All the more important for us, therefore, to make our audiences feel personally welcomed even if they cannot be personally identified. I expect that customers care about customer care. Do centres show that they care about care?

F is also for Finance. Arts people are supposed to be 'no good at money'. Some are not. In my experience, good arts directors or administrators take it in their stride. Arts people are very good at cutting costs – all too often this involves accepting cuts in their own salaries. Arts folk are bad at looking after their own financial interests and none get rich on the process, except some stage directors and a handful of international musical performers who have undoubtedly earned their high fees. Most people work in the arts because they love them. Essentially, they subsidise the arts through their own low earnings. The canard that public funding of the arts provides comfy jobs at generous salaries – usually asserted by those who earn more in a day than the average arts employee does in a week – is a device with which to attack the whole idea of arts subsidy.

G is for Grants. No arts organisation – except Glyndebourne – can live without public grants. Too often the Glyndebourne model – through no fault of its own – is held up as one that others can or should follow. This is a delusion. It is a brilliant financial and artistic special case, a glorious one-off which has evolved over half a century, but has no implications for anyone else. Glyndebourne offers a very specific artistic programme for a specific audience at demanding prices in a carefully tailored environment and during a limited season. All the rest of us rely on grants of one sort or another from government or local government sources.

In the Barbican's case, the sole funder is the Corporation of London. Not content with funding the operations of the Centre, it also matches the Arts Council's grant to the Barbican's resident orchestra, the London Symphony Orchestra, and was until recently a very open-handed 'funder of last resort' to the Royal Shakespeare Company. These direct arts grants, and the additional sums the Corporation gives to academic institutions such as the City's conservatoire – the Guildhall School of Music and Drama – make it the third largest funder of the arts in Britain. Whether grants are a good or a bad thing, see 'Subsidy' below. As the recipient of a particularly generous one, it feels a good idea to me.

H is for Human Resources. Once upon a time we used to call it Personnel. That involved looking after people, but it did not sound sufficiently professional and managerially rigorous. 'Human Resources' all too often suggests that staff are no more than plant and can be as easily declared redundant. Remember, too, that once money turned into 'resources' – in another piece of managerial sleight of hand – there was less of it. So too with human resources: its main aim is to economise on them. HRT usually stands for Hormone Replacement Therapy. In improperly run institutions, HRT stands for 'human replacement theory'. Judge your HR team by whether they really behave like personnel managers.

I is for Ice Creams. Do not underestimate them. They earn money. Many people will buy an ice cream when they will not buy an interval drink, though some people are susceptible to a thick Belgian chocolate bar. Make sure these are part of your total retail offer. Price them correctly. Getting the price right could add a few thousand to your net income. There is a wider moral here: do not irritate your audience, who are not for the greater part well-heeled, by constantly edging up the overall cost of a pleasant evening out. Price sensitivity is not a piece of economics jargon; it means being sensitive about what you charge and not driving members of the public into shrieking, 'ouch, no thanks'. All prices for the supposedly minor items on offer at an arts event should be kept under constant review. When customer resistance is reached – say over the cost of a programme – the signs will be there for all to see. Be sensitive to it.

J is for Jazz. This is an important part of musical programming, a vital part of your programming mix. It can sell very well, at the right quality and in the right quantity. But do not think that jazz audiences are the same as those for pop or rock. Actually – as the broadcasters will tell you – jazz is a very minority taste, important historically but still only appreciated by a few. Presenting it is like adding a sharp spice to your venue: to be used lightly.

K is for Kitchens. They need constant attention on health-and-safety grounds. Nothing gives a venue a bad name so quickly as bad kitchens and – perish the thought – even an outbreak of food poisoning. Time and money spent on them is never wasted.

L is for Lavatories. Same as the above really. The state of the loos is taken by the public as a reliable indicator of the state of health of the institution as a whole. The music may be never so wonderful, the theatre never so sublime, the restaurants never so excellent – if the loos are not kept clean or if they smell, then most of the rest of your good work goes for nothing. I once told a newcomer to the arts management field that a large part of her job would be devoted to kitchens and loos. She thought I was either cynical or mad. A year later she confessed I was all too right.

M is for Marketing. This has become an art as well as a science. A good marketing team will know who the audience is, how they buy their tickets, at what prices, in what size of purchases, where they live and what socio-economic group they come from. They will tell you which ads or press articles brought in which sales. They will tell you who is likely to buy tickets for an event next time, on the basis of who bought them last time. They have a finger on the real pulse of your institution.

And yet. For my taste, it is a shade too mechanistic, too deterministic. While all of us as arts-goers have our preferred artists, our preferred events, I cannot be alone in wanting to be surprised, in wanting to be attracted to the unexpected, the unpredictable, the event that I would not normally go to and that the marketeers could not predict that I would. I have a dream of an audience made up of people who are swept in simply by enthusiasm for an event, not because they came to something like this a year ago. I want audiences of free agents, drawn magnetically by the prospect of quality, driven by free will and not hidebound by who they are, where they live or what they usually see. Marketing is essential – but it should be a guide not a determinant of your actions.

N is for Noise. Sound is good; noise is bad. Sound becomes noise when it is too loud or too intrusive for the person listening.

For instance, the sound of a band playing in the foyers of an arts centre – much advocated to encourage access and informality – becomes noise when it is too blaring or inappropriate for a significant number of others nearby. The sound of casual open-air performances around a centre and the buzz of the audience enjoying them becomes noise to local residents who may dislike the music or may simply dislike the idea of the existence of a centre at all. Monitoring the moment when sound becomes noise demands constant vigilance.

O is for Outreach. Is this the same as Education? Perhaps outreach includes education but goes wider in its attempt to involve the public in the activities of the institution. Outreach also implies a commitment to Access. And to Equality. Does it mean much left to itself? I doubt it but as you will hear the word used a lot then you should be aware of its existence as a portmanteau idea.

P is for Press and Programmes. Be nice to the press but remember that it is not the job of the press to be nice to you. Cultivate journalists by being as open as you can whenever you can. If you succeed, then you have increased the chance that they will trust you or give you the benefit of the doubt when things go wrong. Persuading the press to write feature articles in advance of an event, about a player or a performer, is worth thousands of pounds. As free advertising, it is an essential partner to your marketing strategy. It can persuade people that they should buy tickets. But a review is a review; nothing sells seats like a good one; nothing empties a hall like a group of bad ones.

By Programmes I mean the print the audience buys before entering the auditorium. They are an essential part of your public image. Think about the information you want to present about yourselves and what you do and what part the visitors can play in it. Audiences carry programmes home after the show, read them the following day, leave them lying around thereafter. They are part of your message to the public: here we are, come and join us. Do not let anyone else take control of one of your chief platforms for telling the public about yourselves. Try to make sure that they arrive on time for the show. Always make sure there are enough; running out of programmes leaves only irritated customers.

Q is for Quality. None of us can afford the very best performers providing the very best performances the whole time. But quality-control matters in another way. The audience senses inconsistency of quality. What you offer may not be the very best but it must be very good of its kind. Veering between high quality – when you can afford it – and lesser quality – when you can't – merely sells the audience short. They will notice. Equally, feeding the audiences a steady diet of the very good makes them less tolerant of the merely adequate.

R is for Resources – always insufficient and explained above – and Risk. The two have to be considered together but can never be balanced. Resources are knowable; the level of risk being run with a particular arts programme is notional. Resources are largely fixed; the risk could be limitless. The task is to reduce the risk to the point that it will not destroy the budget. But risk has to be taken or else you do not have an arts programme worth the name. If too little is ventured, then the institution is moribund and the audience will sense the deadly odour of playing safe. On balance, take more rather than less risk, but never shut your eyes to the amount of danger or the consequences of it all coming out on the downside. Be conscious of the financial failure but do not be driven by fear of it. Everyone finds comfort in a *succès d'estime*. Too many such 'successes' may break you.

S is for Sponsors. No organisation can survive without them. British bodies typically find a third of their funding from the public purse, national or local; a third from the takings at the box office; and a third from private, charitable or commercial sponsors. Do not expect sponsors to give money because they feel a duty to do so. 'Philanthropy' has no useful place in the dialogue with them. In the British model of taxation, there is no reason why it should.

They have to be led into a relationship where each side finds that a particular interest is served by co-operating. On the commercial side, such co-operation is frequently driven by the needs of marketing budgets. Arts organisations must be clear what they are providing in return for sponsorship and must be scrupulous and professional in delivering it.

T is for Tourists. We neglect cultural tourism, but it is a growing industry, a high-value industry, an industry that does not pollute the urban environment with coaches, coach fumes and junk-food litter. Stratford-upon-Avon and the Edinburgh Festival apart, the arts world has never co-operated actively and imaginatively among its own branches, never mind with the tourist boards, tour operators and airlines, to sell Britain's myriad cultural activities to foreign visitors. It is an opportunity waiting to be taken up, a great strategic opportunity for boosting sales and raising the image and standing of the arts.

U is for Utopia and the Unexpected. What is an arts utopia? One where everything outlined above has been addressed and realised at the highest possible level; one where the public funding is generous, predictable and proportionately supported by corporate and private sponsorship. A utopia is one where the organisers can offer a varied and balanced mixture of the known, the unknown and the unexpected and where the audience trusts the organisation so much that it takes the unexpected in its stride. Does such a utopia exist? Not that I know. Could it exist? Certainly, which is why the arts must continue to argue without shame or apology for support for what they do.

V is for Vision and Values. Arts organisations are intrinsically unlike business or industry because the commodity they deal with is absolutely unquantifiable. Of course, service and trust are also unquantifiable and lie at the core of many business activities. But then they are qualities that are an essential ingredient in a total measurable product. In the arts, values stand lonely and exposed at the heart of the activity. Without them, there is no activity. The vision expresses what they are. If you cannot imagine your vision, then express your vision in words, the values will never be understood or realised.

W is for the Wonder that, given all the obstacles and snares, any play is mounted, any concert is played at all, still more at the levels of quality that are achieved. Wonder is what you hope the audiences will feel at the end of a performance, when they contemplate the greatness of a work and the brilliance with which it was realised.

X is for Extending the audience's choice so that their experience of the arts is constantly refreshed and renewed, and the arts themselves do not slip back into the merely tried and trusted, which soon becomes the old and rejected.

Y is for Youth, the audience of the future. You must respect youth, accommodate it and learn from it. Do not appease youth, especially when it says that something is 'too boring', 'too difficult' or 'not relevant'. Much damage has been done to the arts, and to the young, by the educational system bending before these time-honoured reactions of the intellectually immature. You do no favour to the young by pretending that the arts are easier than they are or by adapting them to iron out the difficulties and at the same time removing the richness, the ambiguities and the complexity which are the only things that make the arts worthwhile.

Z is for Zing and Zip, the qualities that are needed in the arts to keep going through the alphabet of duties and responsibilities and obligations, the struggle for resources and sponsorship and access, and all the other letters of the arts alphabet.

If you can use all the letters of this alphabet in running an arts institution, then you have the ingredients for conducting a literate dialogue with your audience, your funders and yourselves.

Afterword: Art and Culture – Old Responsibilities, New Rhetoric?

Imagine the Sea of Galilee. It is seven o'clock in the morning. The water is dead flat, bath-warm, dragonflies darting around at eye-level, the surrounding hills already shrouded in a September haze. The silence and the water are slightly parted by the genteel breaststrokes of British arts leaders. The occasional group stands chest deep musing over some mutual concern. Most do not. We take the soul-easing silence as a gift, a precious moment of preparation for the discussions to come. Make no mistake about it, a colloquium is shaped by its surroundings and this one was transformed by them.

I had expected to be entranced by the Sea and hills of Galilee. No one can be indifferent to the knowledge that these were the hills that Jesus and the Disciples walked, the waters that they fished, the villages where they met, taught, broke bread and began the prophesied journey to Jerusalem. But these are not 'heritage' tourist sites for the devout – though some are treated with more sensitivity than others – and they spoke to many of us in a way that was heart-catchingly quietening.

And it was not only the great Christian landmarks that cast their spell over us. The drive up the Golan Heights, the view from the top commanding the whole of Galilee, the knowledge that some of our Israeli co-locutors lost most of their best friends in the fighting, this too put our everyday thoughts into a deeper, contemporary perspective. For the physical setting of the discussions and the incredible wrenching of the imagination involved in moving across two millennia of history in a few hours played their essential part in making our discussions what they were.

The subject of the Anglo-Israeli Colloquium could not have been more fundamental, nor more appropriate as a topic for the closing thoughts in this book. 'Art and Culture – Whose Responsibility?' lays the question starkly before us. Unless someone accepts responsibility for art and culture, then their continued existence cannot be taken for granted. Israelis and Britons alike, we recognised a shared concern in our conversations, felt a common anguish, sought a mutual determination not to avoid the issue. If we did not find solutions, we felt that we at least indicated to ourselves some new ways ahead. I hope they offer the chance of escaping from some of the deadlocks within which we struggle in the everyday lives of the arts.

In most discussions about the arts and culture, still more so about the way they should be paid for, there is a reluctant consensus that the arts should exist in a healthy society. If such a consensus does exist, then it is only the start of the debate. The arts do not exist in a vacuum; they have to be willed into viable financial existence. Who does the willing? Who does the paying? Whose responsibility is it for the arts and culture to exist, better still to flourish? What are the respective roles of government, business, the people, and the arts themselves to create and sustain a vital artistic environment? That is what we discussed at Galilee.

Too often, these questions are answered – by arts people – using the 'should' form of the verb; thus the government, or business, or the voters 'should' fund the arts because the arts are useful and deserving and absolutely valuable in their own terms. While it is very easy to slip into a world of 'shoulds' and 'oughts', the fact is that such vocabulary impresses and persuades no one; these terms of implied obligation on the part of others butter absolutely no financial parsnips. The debate must take place without them.

Of course, the government has 'a' responsibility to foster the arts. This is not a sole or exclusive responsibility and it is heavily modified by practical questions about funding. If government is wise, it will shoulder that responsibility, for all the usually adduced reasons ranging from education, to tourism, to economic and urban regeneration, employment and even basic national self-respect. These are all the practical, mundane, contingent reasons for supporting art. This is government acting in a matter-of-fact, practical manner. But the trend to do it in partnership with others is growing and in keeping with the way we think about plural, decentralised societies today.

Audiences, too, have a real responsibility for keeping art and culture alive; without people, visitors, listeners and viewers, performances, events or exhibitions are dead. Business has a responsibility too, one that is imperfectly defined and inconsistently acknowledged. If arts and culture rely on this tripod of responsibility – state, people, business – it is a pretty unstable one, with each leg behaving as if it has a mind of its own, and often looking ungainly and precarious since each is of a different length and strength from the others. The idea of a 'shared' responsibility is over-ambitious. Even to say that each of these three elements has a responsibility is only to begin the discussion, not end it.

But there is another constituency whose responsibility for art and culture is often taken for granted or overlooked altogether – the broadcasters. Half a generation ago, the presence of the arts on the main terrestrial radio and television networks was palpable. The great landmark TV series of art were national events, part of a national dialogue, an expression of shared values and assumptions. Now arts programmes are peripheral, marginalised, weakened by the new laws of obligation to the marketplace. You would expect that of ITV. You would not expect it of the BBC, the second largest funder of the arts in Britain, and still the largest cultural influence in the nation. The BBC's new (self-imposed) market obligation is to maximise its audiences on all its networks at all times. This is a monstrous *trahison des clercs*, meaning as it does that programmes will not be judged on their intrinsic quality but rather on the size of the audiences they can deliver. The devastating impact of this attitude on the BBC's programming and thereafter on the national perception of and understanding about the the arts is still being weighed and is yet to be fully felt.

The way the government looks at the arts is coloured and informed by the prevailing atmosphere in which we live – a post-modernist world where nothing is good or bad (only 'appropriate' or 'inappropriate' depending on circumstances), where everyone's opinion is as good as everyone else's, and value judgements have been relativised to the point of non-existence. There is no overriding political and social consensus on which a government can easily and comfortably base an arts policy. For politicians to assert that such a foundation exists demands a degree of confidence and reflects a wish to lead that the world of focus groups and media sensitivity renders unfashionable when it is not downright politically imprudent. Such confidence is increasingly rare in the prevailing atmosphere of millennial tension.

The world of those who work in the arts must play its part too. Increasingly, there is a robust readiness to stop defending the indefensible and to be ready to admit that some artistic activities are bad. Arts funders, even their peer groups, need to be ready to tell a wannabe dance company that they are not good enough to warrant funding as a full-time, independent dance group; or to tell an ethnic arts group that their work might be satisfying in an anthropological way, might have a certain local, social value, but fails by the artistic standards applied to others. Or to tell yet another would-be start-up symphony orchestra that London, for instance, has too many already. Picking winners in the arts may be a precarious business; but hanging on to losers becomes a bad habit.

While the business/commercial sector is now – in Britain – a significant funder of the arts, no one can say it 'should' perform that role. We have learned that companies have a weak sense of supporting the arts for reasons of pure 'philanthropy' – a word that is almost forbidden to use – and a strong sense of doing so for commercial, market-driven or PR reasons. We have come to accept, through long and perhaps bitter experience, that it is a waste of time approaching most companies with really risky or experimental artistic ventures. The answer to such proposals is all too often negative: 'Our clients would not be interested in seeing such and such.' In 1997, the English National Opera could find no one to sponsor their ambitious production of Zimmerman's *Die Soldaten*, admittedly not an ingratiating work but clearly an event of real artistic importance. If such conservatism, in the eyes of some, is a kind of commercially-driven censorship of artistic activity in everything but name, we take it as a fact of life. No one can be coerced into backing something they do not like.

For the arts do live in the marketplace, the challenging marketplace of public and private taste. They live with the disciplines and judgements of the box office, they face the verdicts and acclaim of criticism. Engaging business in funding the arts places them still more in arenas where purely arts-driven wishes are subjected to the scrutiny and evaluation of others with very different sets of values. Never before have the arts had to justify themselves and explain themselves more than they do today.

Where does this leave the responsibility of the people, to use an old-fashioned word – the audience, after all, is an altogether smaller subset of the larger group, the people, the voters, the public-at-large, call them what you will. Are the arts accountable to people – as distinct from audiences – in a democratic way? Where does democracy interpose itself in the relationship between the artist/performer and those who pay to watch and attend, or are taxed to enable the performance to take place?

In the general openness and candour generated by the spirit of Galilee, we admitted to a certain unease about the audience. 'We are afraid of audiences,' suggested one participant. 'We are afraid of giving things to people who do not know.' Why is this? Two immediate thoughts arise. Why do people not know about the arts? Or are we anxious about the length of time it would take to explain what needs explanation?

There was another observation: 'The audience wants more of what it knows and less of what it does not know.' Clearly, if this were true, there would be no way out along this road, one where everyone was condemned to a hellish eternity of recycling the familiar and avoiding anything that smacked of the different or the strange.

There was a way out of this creative and spiritual dead end, and we were drawn to it by looking closely at the particular experience of dance – not classical ballet, but modern dance. In Britain, with the creation of many new companies, an entirely new audience has emerged – one that is classless, often with a strong ethnic base, and one that is not afraid of modern music. This sudden burgeoning came about through clear policy direction from the Arts Council, and the strong creative leadership of some notably gifted individuals. This fortunate congruence of influences produced a consensus between creator, funder and audience, and one where – in one key comment – 'the success of these performers and performances did not depend on the communication of the whole.' What this meant was that you did not have to defend or advocate modern dance as a whole; you were simply invited to enjoy and admire a particular example of that art. But each particular success had the effect of advancing the cause of the whole. Each new company drove forward the form of contemporary dance by its own innovations. It did not have to make the case for the entire activity of dance and ballet as it did so. And yet the impact of a number of successful companies on a case-by-case basis created the awareness of and support for the entire genre of modern dance.

If that was true, the example of dance offered a case-study of the way in which artistic innovation and public consent could co-exist and march hand in hand. At the heart of this case-study lay the key experience of 'leadership'. What sort of leadership? Arts institutions must be more democratic, or at least more accountable (the idea of how this democracy works in this context still has to be teased out), but artistic creation – the responsibility to innovate, to renew, to develop – must lie with the performers and creators. This was not an arrogation of power, but represented an assumption of responsibility. After all, as one observer warned, 'the arts have nothing to do with democracy – but the arts have always been good at limiting tyranny.'

Four words summed up the rather solitary responsibility the arts have to shoulder, in the view of one participant: 'Leadership, reference, delivery and courage.'

If leadership and courage are called for, how brave are we in

shouldering our responsibilities to the arts? Brave in speaking up
and speaking out! 'Of course we have convictions,' said one
participant, and an event like this allowed us to air these
convictions, 'but we lack courage to speak out for those
convictions in the wider public domain.' Why is this? It struck
me that there are many reasons for failing to stand up for what
we believe in. Perhaps we are embarrassed by our acceptance of
public and business funding; we are challenged by the rhetoric,
vigour and practice of the market; we are too easily run ragged by
the arcane vocabulary and abstruse practices of management
consultants; we are wounded by charges of 'elitism' against which
we have no effective verbal counter; and when we do throw back
charges of 'philistinism', the charge of superiority and snobbish-
ness undoes us yet again.

We are fearful of rejection, deeply threatened by the indifference of the under-thirty-five generation, for whom culture equals
lifestyle and the behaviour and the outward symbols of fashion
and display; for whom the activities of the Internet, rock-and-
roll, drugs, films, TV and clubbing provide a feast of involvement
and engagement that we might call 'entertainment' but that they
know is 'culture' – their culture. How can we overcome such
indifference merely by speaking out against it? And the worst of
it is that they have stolen our word into the bargain. Instead of
culture defining the finest aspirations, the greatest achievements,
the best thoughts of society, it has been debased to a mere
description of how people live and behave, good, bad or
indifferent.

But the dialogue must start with the indifferent, the unknow-
ing, the agnostic, the unpersuaded, the downright hostile. The
dialogue must take place on terms defined by the arts world
because it is our existence that is under threat. First, by offering
our audiences a new deal, not a financial one but a new deal of
partnership. One colleague expressed it in this way: 'Give people
what they will like. But give them things they could not judge
beforehand.' This takes a little de-coding but I take it to mean
that the arts should want the audiences to like what they put on,
but the audiences should trust that what they may like in

practice is often not something that they could predict before-hand.

This idea of the extended hand of partnership went further: 'Help us to judge what goes on,' suggested one. I think that, unconsciously perhaps, this phrase 'what goes on' includes a double invitation – 'that which is taking place at an event' and also 'that which is put on in the first place': in other words, become a true partner in the activity. We did not believe that market research could tell us what arts events to put on – but we were looking ahead to a situation where the interaction with the public was such that some sense of what the audience was ready to take would become part of the artistic planning process. But the audience had to play a more active part than that of a sheet anchor slowing down the artistic drive of creativity and innovation.

'But all this is too dreary,' objected one member. 'No one is speaking about enjoyment.' He was immediately corrected. 'What the arts are offering is joy as well as enjoyment,' a more complex idea. Another reminded us of the inscription over the entrance to the Danish Royal Ballet – 'Not only for Pleasure'.

But we were dogged by a realisation that the old terms of the artistic debate are no longer helpful. Old assumptions have been passed by. As one participant said: 'In the past, there was a consensus about the arts and culture that was summed up by the saying: "However few it served, it helped the rest." ' We could no longer rely on that as an assertion that could command agreement, respect or funding. Many would – rightly or wrongly – simply walk away from the idea as patronising and exclusive. So we had to try and move ahead. The arts needed a 'new rhetoric to express and enshrine old principles'. Perhaps it could be found in the awareness that as intellectual disciplines change, reform and alter their boundaries, as understanding of the world requires an altogether new set of inter-disciplinary approaches, so the arts would become an essential ingredient in understanding the vastly changing world all around us and in explaining it. Far from being marginalised and at the edges of contemporary understanding, the arts would be seen as central in binding together a world otherwise destined for disintegration.

What words and phrases could be devised to shape and articulate this new rhetoric of justification for the arts. Here are some random key-phrases that emerged. The arts are about 'understanding the world'. Their most valuable function is 'taking people out of themselves', about 'seeing the other side of the mountain', about 'getting past the screen', as a way of 'making connections between people'. Some were grimmer: 'Ignorance is not much fun – and not much use either.' Perhaps the best was also the most affirmative, banishing elitism and embracing inclusiveness: 'The best for the best is the best for all.'

At Galilee, this group of people veered between optimism and pessimism, depression and excitement, realism and broad visions. My own conclusion is that in a tight corner, there is no room for pessimism, depression and realism. Such feelings will never get you out of it. A reaffirmation of principles must be a part of the new rhetoric, which itself needs to be founded on a new self-belief. An unqualified belief in excellence; a commitment to absolute standards; a deep caution about invasive relativism; and a sure sense that the sheer revelation and understanding that the arts have always offered and continue to provide will sooner rather than later persuade more than the already committed that Art Matters.